August 30, 2007

Dear Dolores

Irish Blessings on your birthday!
Thank you for blessing me with the
gift of your friendship. Love,
Pat xoxo

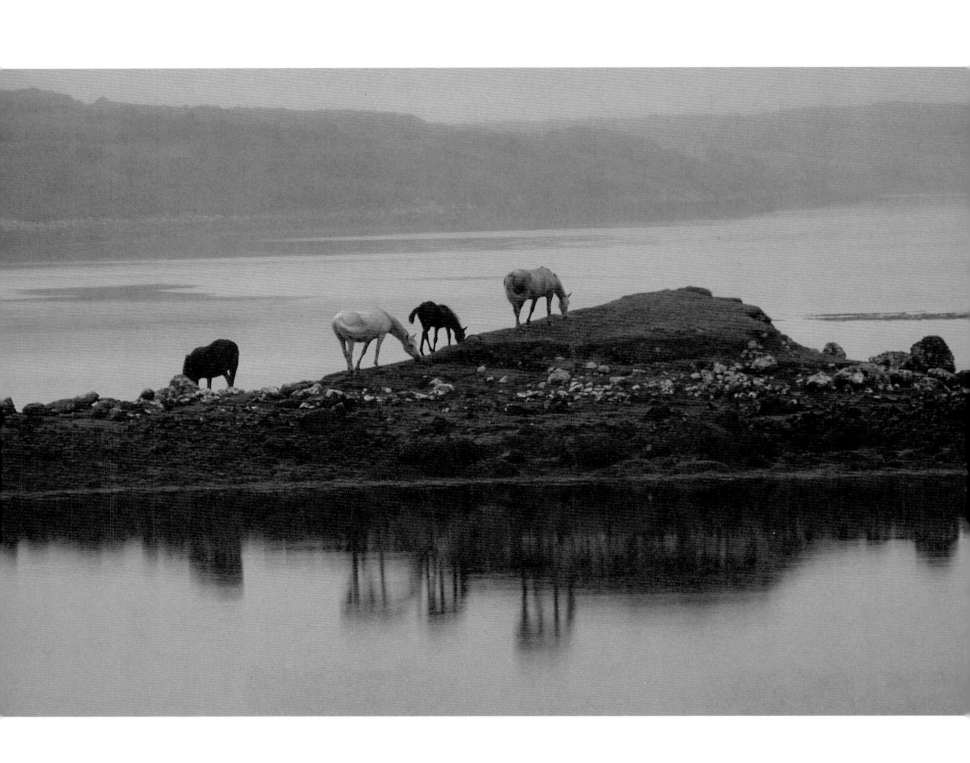

Irish Blessings

A Photographic Celebration

Collected with an Introduction by Ashley Shannon

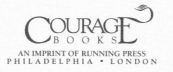

AN IMPRINT OF RUNNING PRESS
PHILADELPHIA • LONDON

9   8   7
Digit on the right indicates the number of this printing

Library of Congress Cataloging-in-Publication Number 98-072369

ISBN 0-7624-0478-7

Cover and interior design by Frances J. Soo Ping Chow
Photo research by Susan Oyama
Edited by Brendan J. Cahill
Typography: ITC Berkeley

Published by Courage Books, an imprint of
Running Press Book Publishers
125 South Twenty-second Street
Philadelphia, Pennsylvania 19103-4399

Visit us on the web! www.runningpress.com

Contents

Introduction

The Irish have always been a spiritual people—even before St. Patrick arrived to convert them to Christianity in the fifth century. Warmth and kindness, generosity and goodwill invigorate the spiritual heritage of Ireland, and all of these traits are preserved in the traditional blessings featured in this book, which have been passed down from generation to generation among Irish families and spread throughout the world by Irish missionaries and emigrants.

The Irish landscape is itself a blessing. From the rolling fields of Munster to the gentle hills of Killarney, from the spectacular coastal scenery of the Dingle Peninsula to the desolate northern beauty of Connemara, Ireland deserves its reputation as one of the loveliest of countries. It's said that forty shades of green are found among the fields and vales of Ireland and any visitor can see why. Even on the greyest of days, Ireland's greens seem to glow with a life of their own: the soft moss growing on crumbling stone walls, the verdant lawns surrounding the country estates, the dark ivy creeping on cottages—all of these are variations on a lush theme which weaves itself into a symphony of color.

The intensity of the landscape of the Emerald Isle has conquered the hearts of people around the world, even those who are "Irish" only on St. Patrick's Day. Ireland holds power over the imagination like no other land, offering to each person an opportunity to discover an individual sense of beauty. Whether one prefers the austere beauty of a ruined monastery buried deep in the Tipperary countryside or the bustle and Georgian splendor of Dublin's streets, Ireland has as many personalities as it does shades of green.

This book captures the beauty of the island in all its moods. The blessings and poems express the good humor and generous hospitality that are essential parts of the Irish character—not to mention the poetic turn of phrase or occasional irreverent witticism so distinctive to Irish writing. The accompanying pictures evoke the landscape where these traits were forged. Together with the invocation for "soft rain and easy roads" in the best-known of Irish blessings, or W. B. Yeats's homage to the call of his lake isle while standing on the "pavements grey," they capture the eternal essence of the holy land of Ireland.

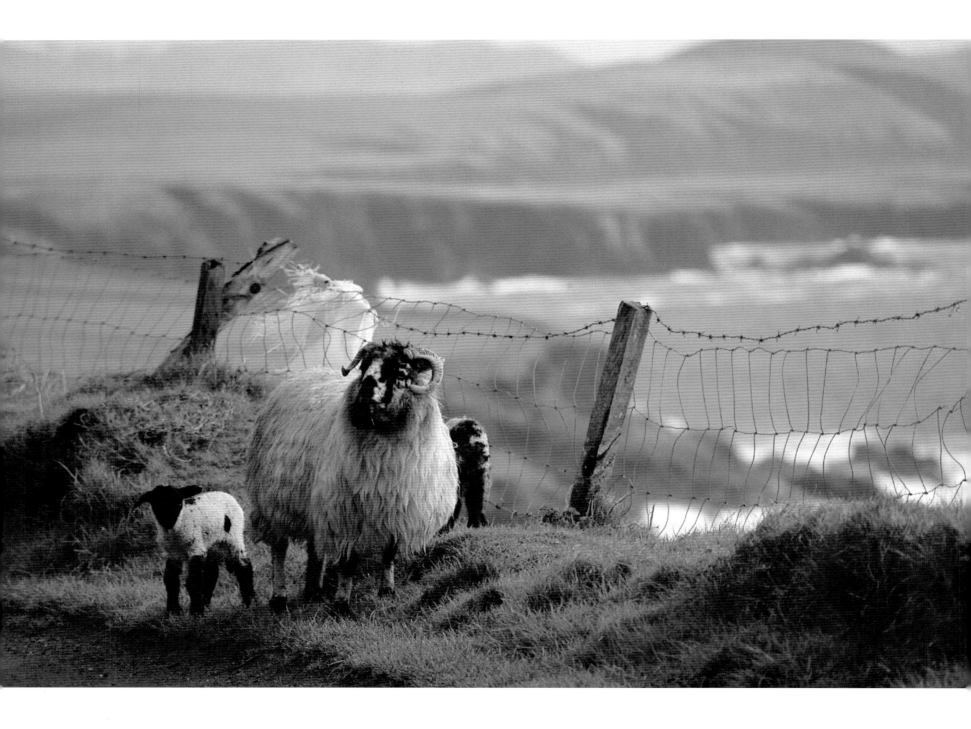

Blessings from
the Land of Eire

I am of Ireland

And of the holy land of Ireland

Good sir I pray of ye

For saintly charity

Come dance with me

In Ireland.

ANONYMOUS
14TH-CENTURY IRISH POET

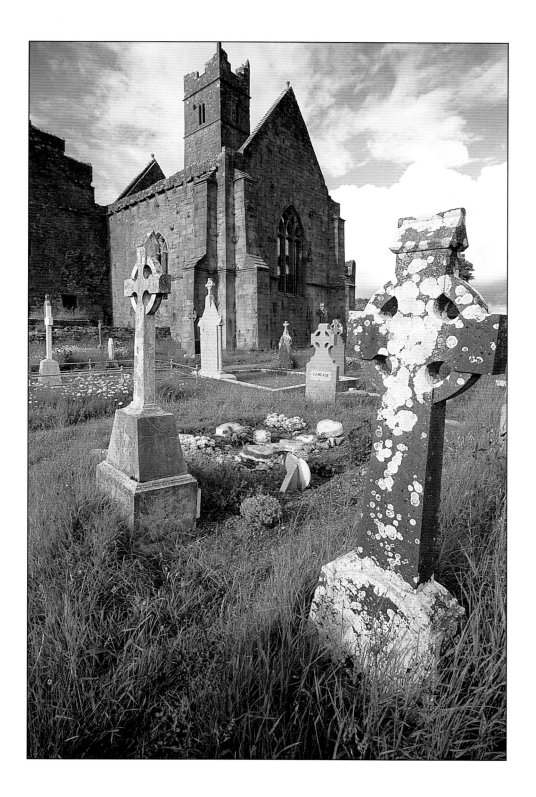

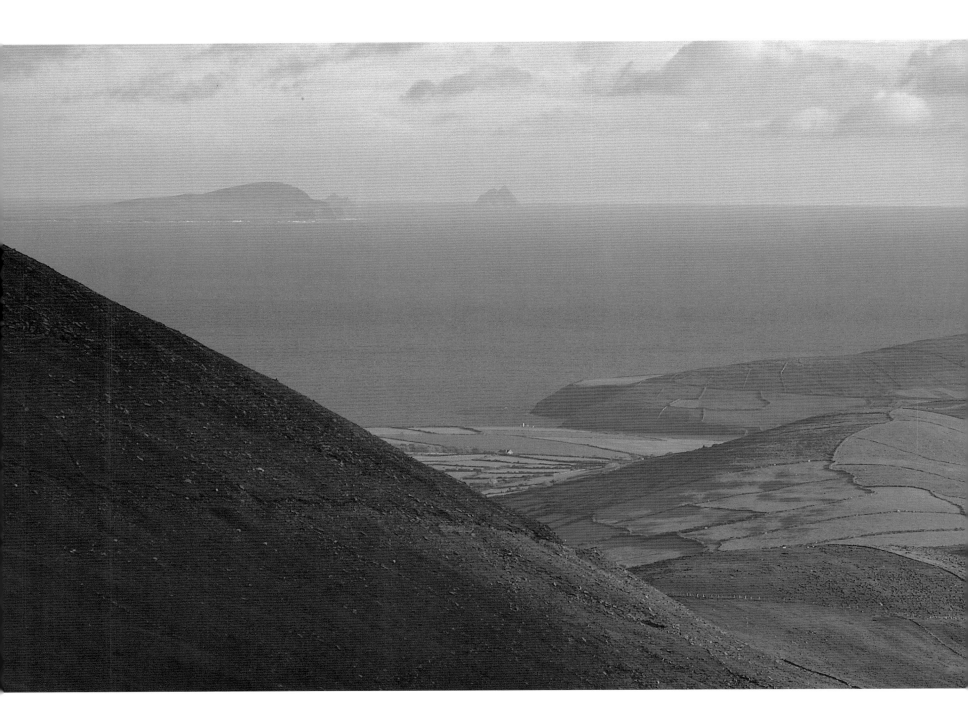

MAY THE IRISH HILLS

CARESS YOU.

MAY HER LAKES AND RIVERS

BLESS YOU.

MAY THE LUCK OF THE IRISH

ENFOLD YOU.

MAY THE BLESSINGS OF SAINT PATRICK

BEHOLD YOU.

An old Irish recipe for longevity:

Leave the table hungry.

Leave the bed sleepy.

Leave the table thirsty.

Ireland,

it's the one place on earth

That heaven has kissed

With melody, mirth,

And meadow and mist.

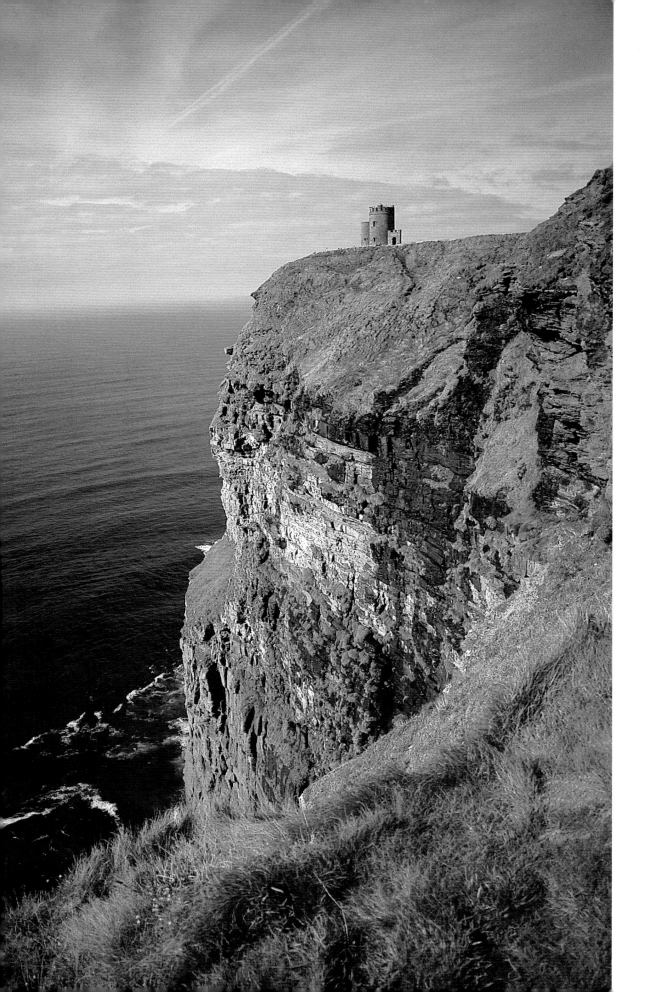

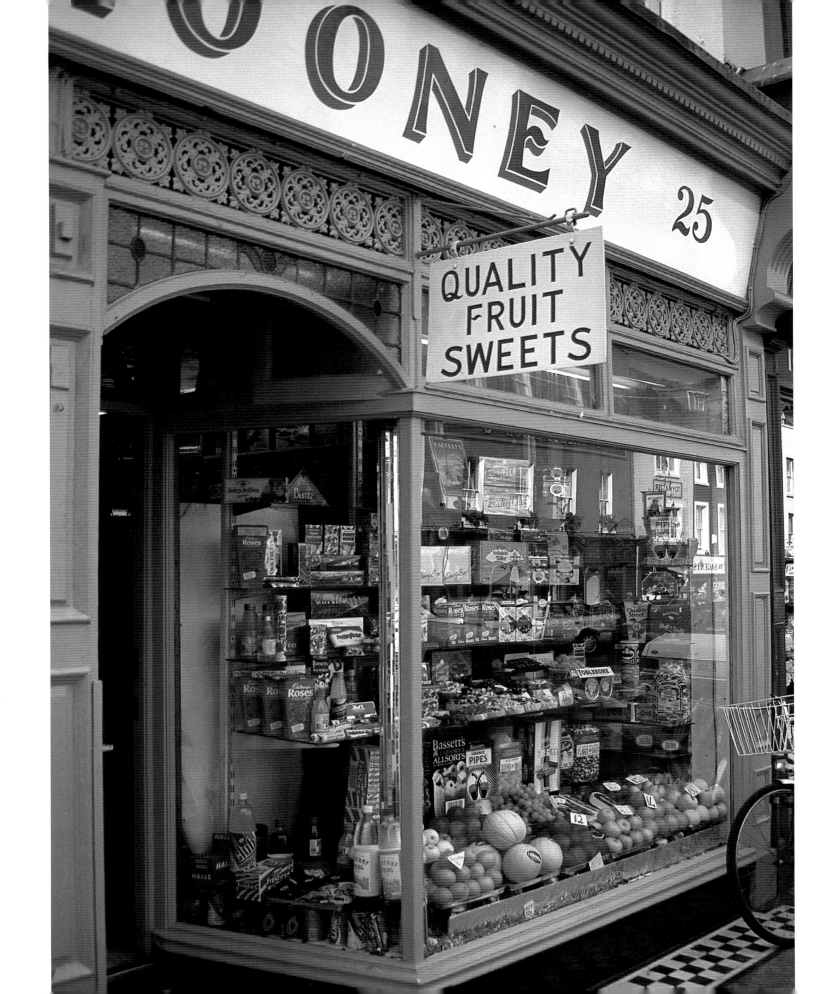

May your heart be warm and happy

With the lilt of Irish laughter

Every day in every way

And forever and ever after.

ay the luck of the Irish be always at hand,

And good friends always near you.

May each and every coming day

Bring some special joy to cheer you.

Now sweetly lies old Ireland,

Emerald green beyond the foam,

Awakening sweet memories,

Calling the heart back home.

EIRE

Where the wind has a sound like a sweet song,

And anyone can hum it,

And the heather grows upon the hills

And shamrocks not far from it.

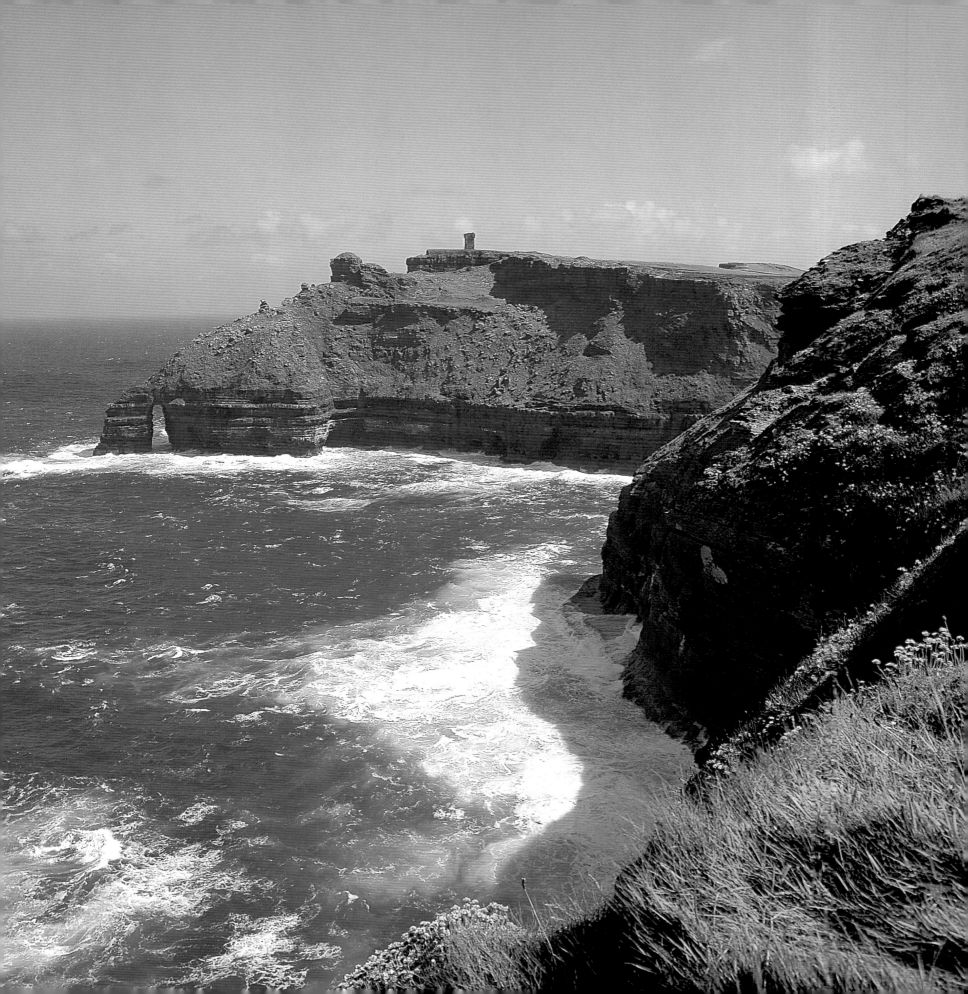

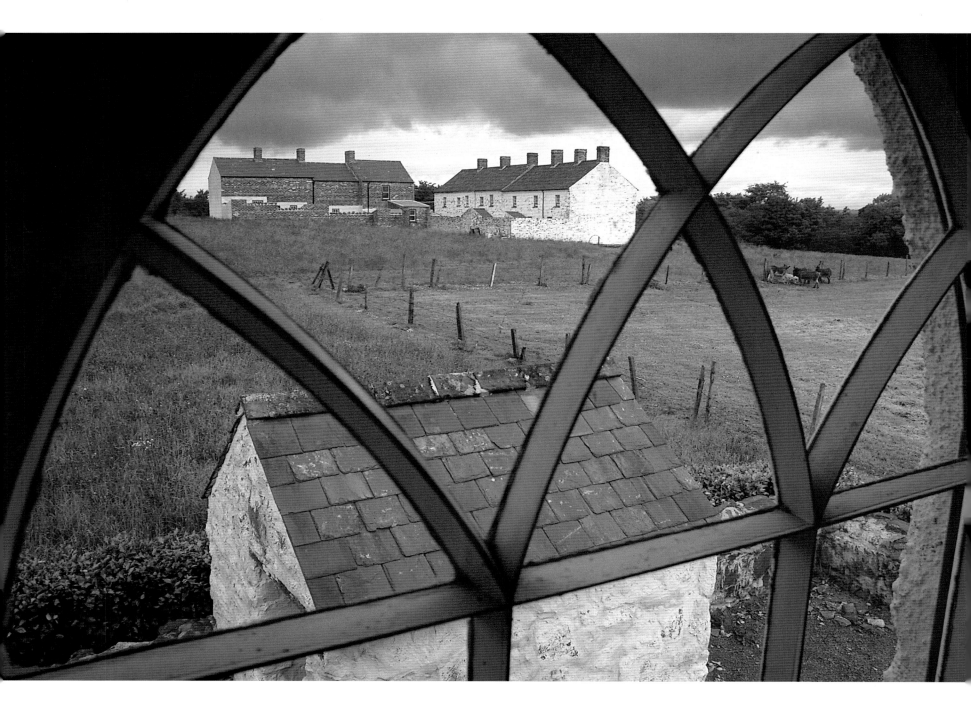

ST. PATRICK'S BREASTPLATE

Christ be with me,

Christ be within me,

Christ behind me, Christ before me,

Christ beside me, Christ to win me,

Christ to comfort me, Christ above me,

Christ in quiet, Christ in danger,

Christ in hearts of all that love me,

Christ in mouth of friend and stranger.

St. Patrick
5th-century Irish cleric

When Irish eyes are smiling,

Sure it's like a morning spring.

In the lilt of Irish laughter

You can hear the angels sing.

When Irish hearts are happy,

All the world seems bright and gay.

And when Irish eyes are smiling,

They'll steal your heart away!

Traditional Irish Folk Song

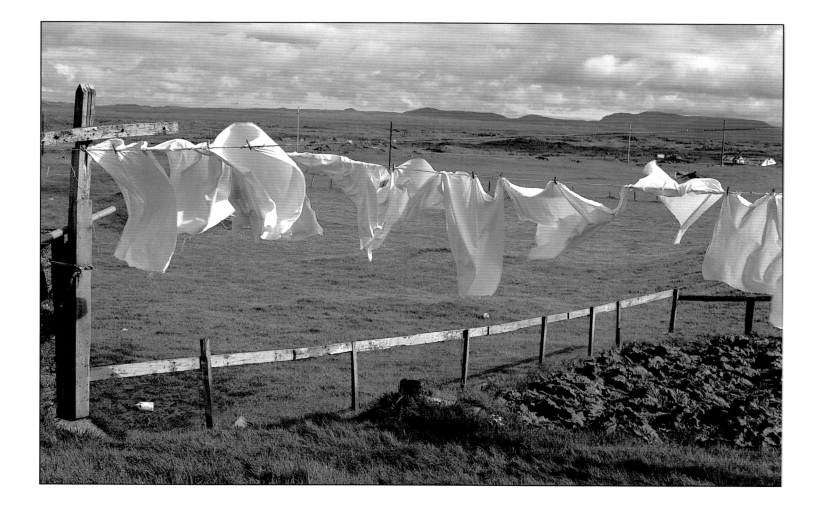

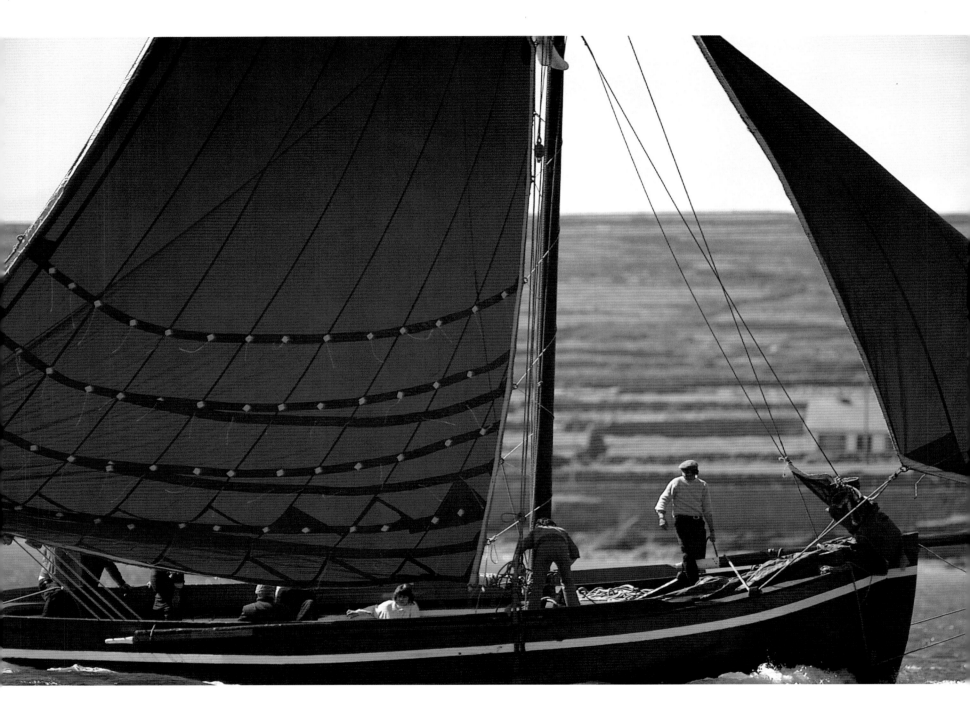

The savage loves his native shore,

    Though rude the soil and chill the air;

Well then may Erin's sons adore

    Their isle, which nature formed so fair!

What flood reflects a shore so sweet,

    As Shannon great, or past'ral Bann?

Or who a friend or foe can meet,

    As generous as an Irishman?

JAMES ORR
IRISH POET (1770–1816)

May Ireland's voice be ever heard,

    Amid the world's applause!

And never be her flag-staff stirred

    But in an honest cause!

THOMAS DAVIS
IRISH POET (1814–1845)

A FRUITFUL CLIME IS EIRE'S, THROUGH VALLEY, MEADOW, PLAIN,

AND IN THE FAIR LAND OF EIRE, O!

THE VERY 'BREAD OF LIFE' IS IN THE YELLOW GRAIN

ON THE FAIR HILLS OF EIRE, O!

FAR DEARER TO ME THAN THE TONES MUSIC YIELDS,

IS THE LOWING OF THE KINE AND THE CALVES IN HER FIELDS

AND THE SUNLIGHT THAT SHONE LONG AGO ON THE SHIELDS

OF THE GAELS, ON THE FAIR HILLS OF EIRE, O!

James Clarence Mangan
Irish poet (1803–1849)

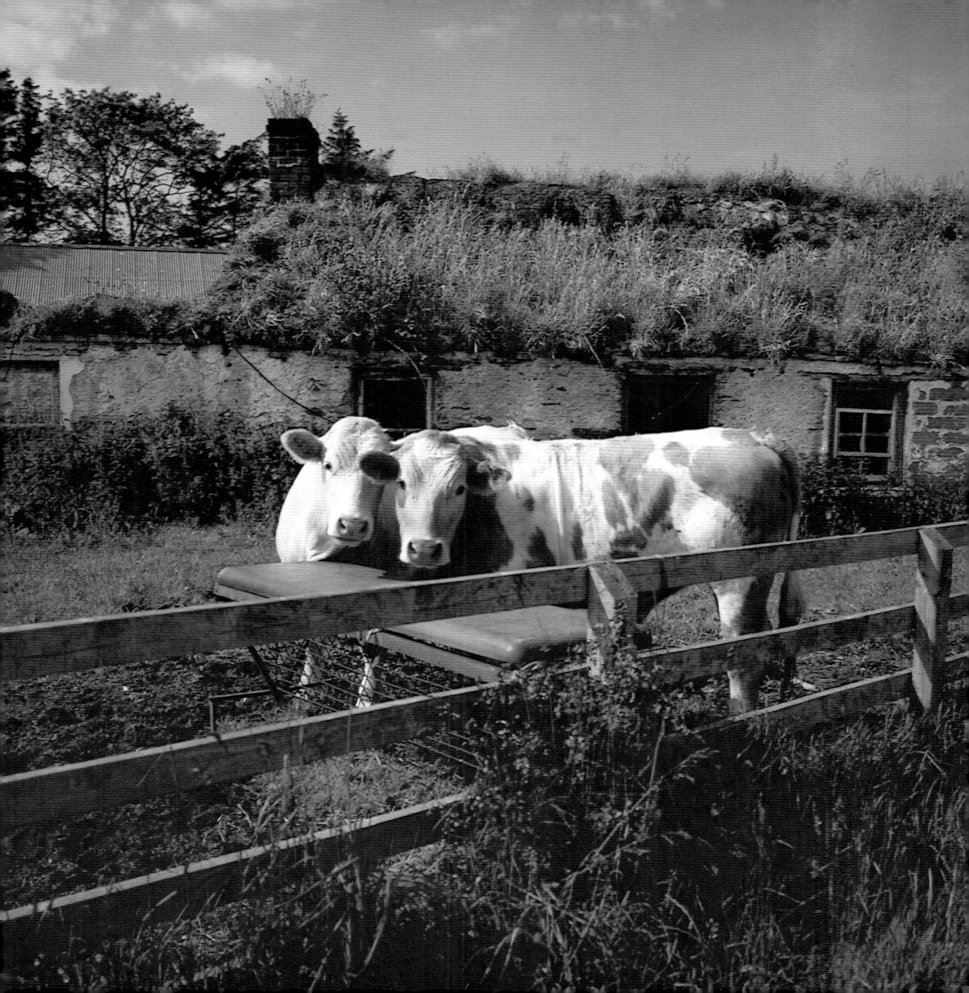

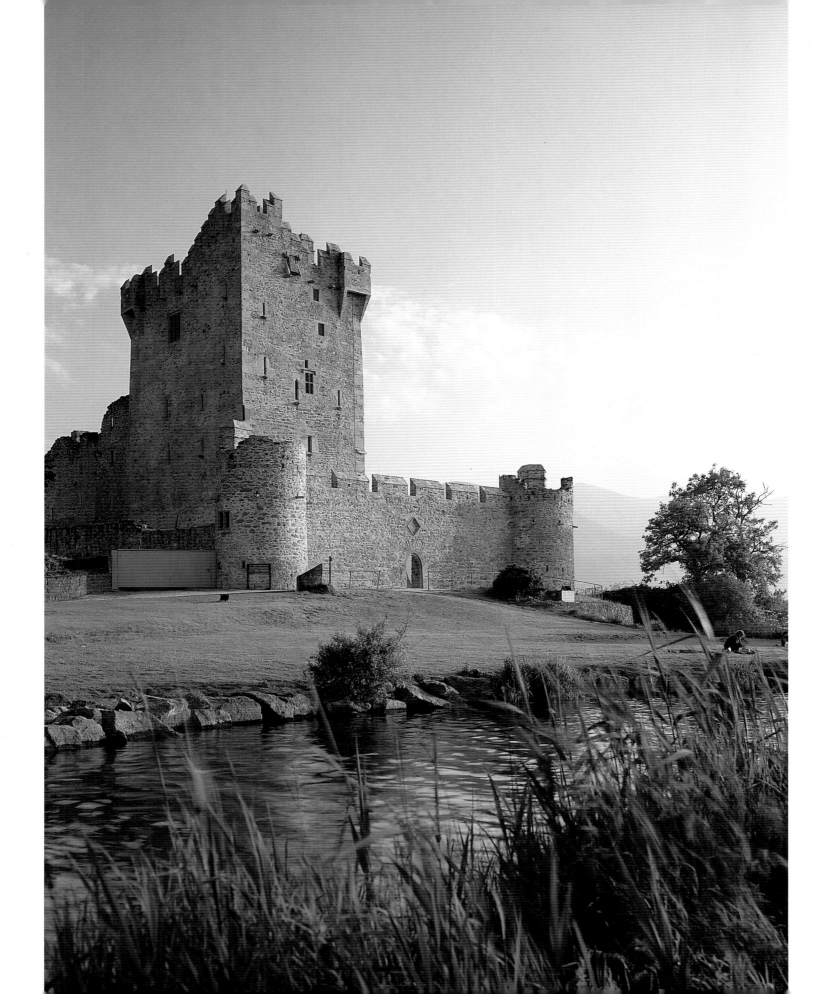

LOV'D LAND OF THE BARDS AND SAINTS! TO ME

THERE'S NOUGHT SO DEAR AS THY MINSTRELSY;

BRIGHT IS NATURE'S EVERY DRESS,

RICH IN UNBORROWED LOVELINESS;

WINNING IS EVERY SHAPE SHE WEARS,

WINNING IS SHE IN THY OWN SWEET AIRS . . .

Thomas Furlong
Irish poet (1794–1827)

The pillar towers of Ireland, how wondrously they stand

By the lakes and rushing rivers through the valleys of our land

In mystic file, through the isle, they lift their heads sublime,

These gray old pillar temples, these conquerors of time!

DENIS MCCARTHY
IRISH POET (1817–1882)

Were you ever in Tipperary, where the fields are so sunny and green,

And the heath-brown Slieve-bloom and the Galtees look down with so proud a mien?

'Tis there you would see more beauty than is on all Irish ground—

God bless you, my sweet Tipperary, for where could your match be found?

Mary Kelly
Irish poet (1825–1910)

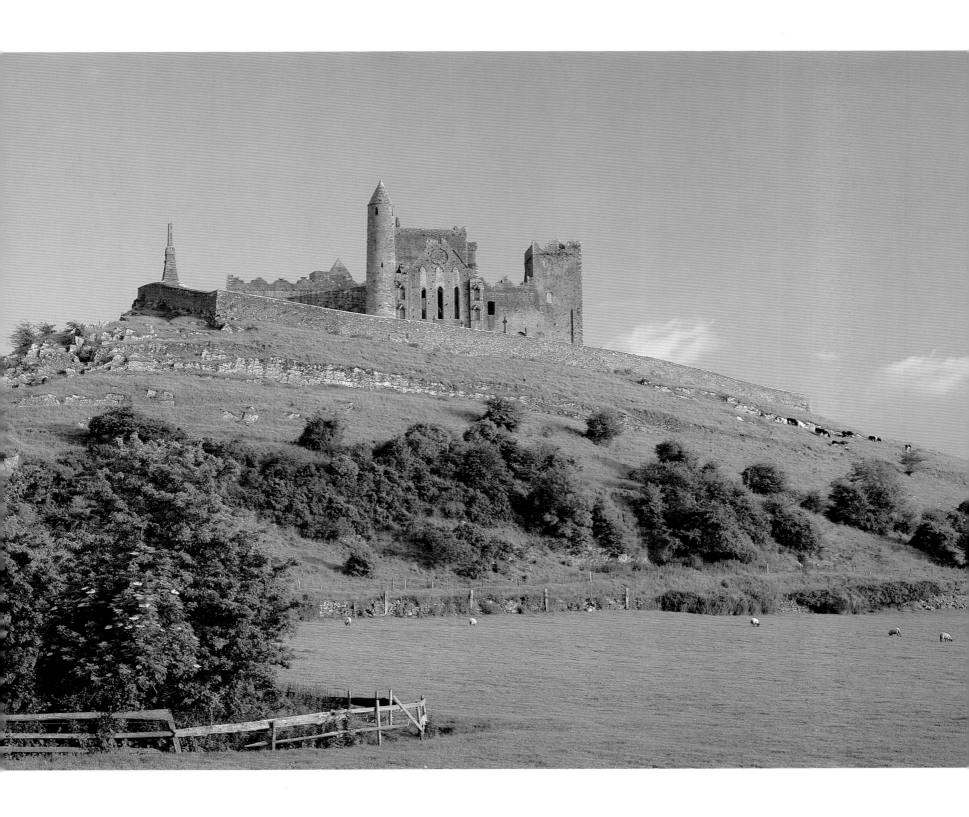

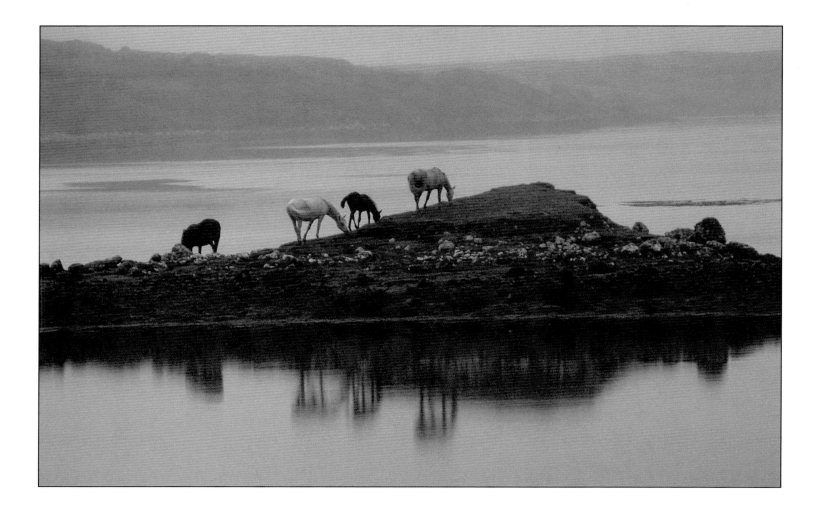

When Erin first rose from the dark swelling flood

God bless'd the Emerald Isle, and saw it was good;

The em'rald of Europe, it sparked and shone—

In the ring of the world, the most precious stone.

WILLIAM DRENNAN
IRISH POET (1754–1820)

She is a rich and rare land,

Oh, she's a fresh and fair land;

She is a dear and rare land,

this native land of mine.

Thomas Davis
Irish poet (1814–1845)

MAY THE SAINTS PROTECT YE—

AN' SORROW NEGLECT YE,

AN' BAD LUCK TO THE ONE

THAT DOESN'T RESPECT YE!

T' ALL THAT BELONG TO YE,

AN LONG LIFE T' YER HONOR—

THAT'S THE END OF MY SONG T' YE!

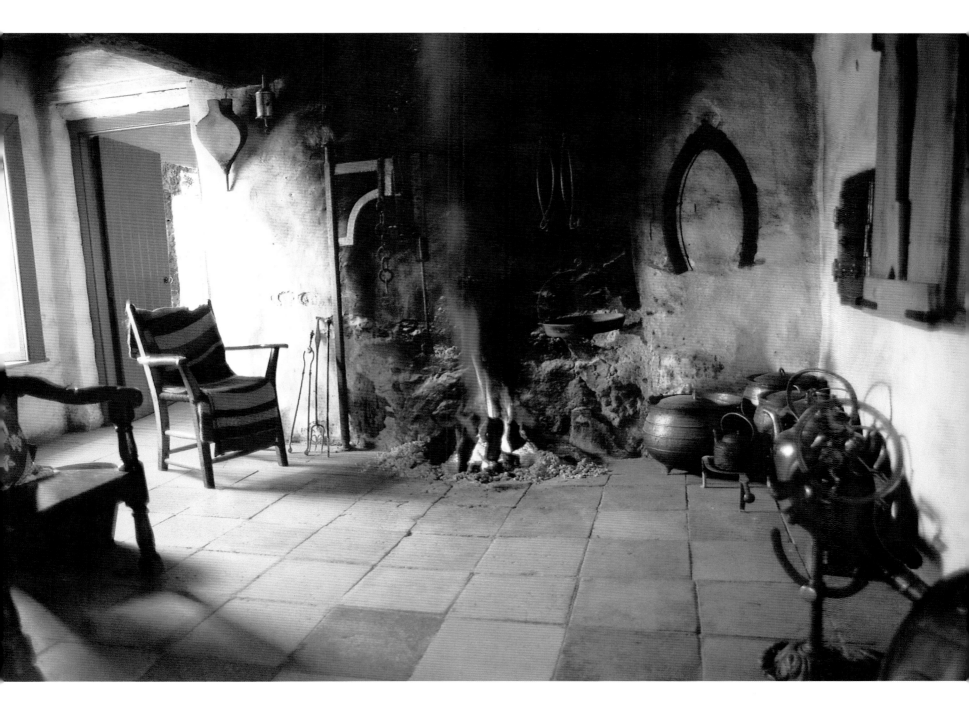

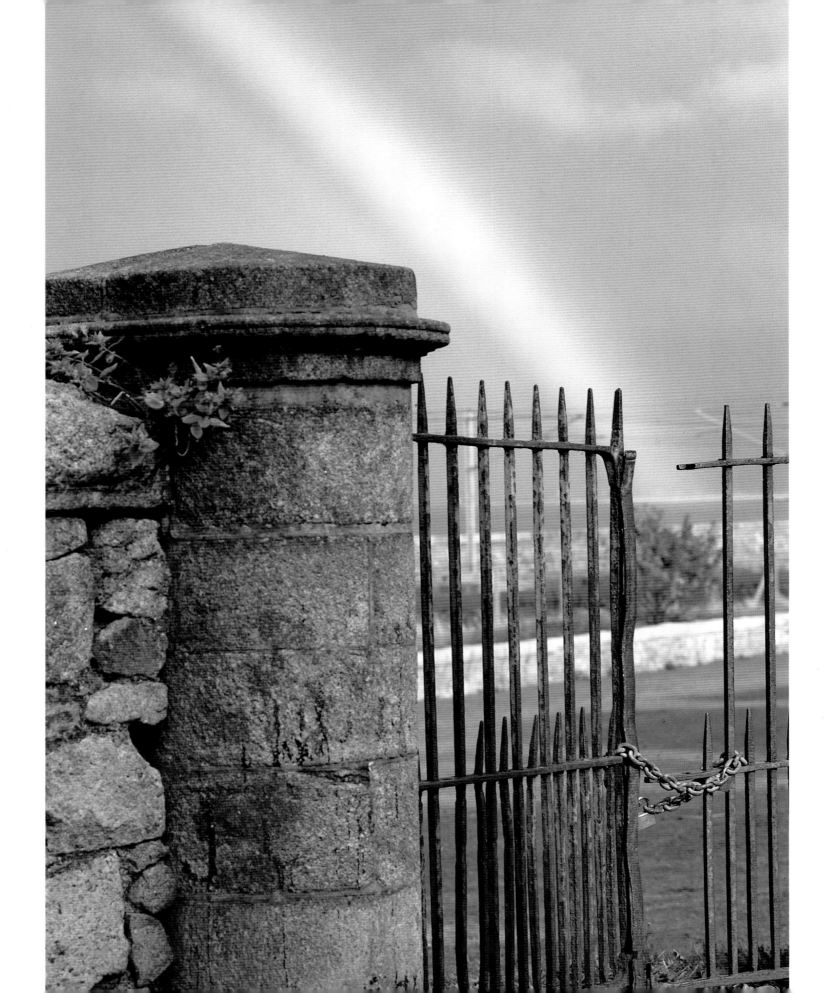

May your thoughts be as glad as the shamrocks.

May your heart be as light as a song.

May each day bring you bright happy hours,

That stay with you all year long.

For each petal on the shamrock

This brings a wish your way—

Good health, good luck, and happiness

For today and every day.

MAY YOUR BLESSINGS OUTNUMBER

THE SHAMROCKS THAT GROW,

AND MAY TROUBLE AVOID YOU

WHEREVER YOU GO.

When the first light of sun—

When the long day is done—

In your smiles and your tears—

Through each day of your years—

May you always have these blessings . . .

A soft breeze when summer comes,

A warm fireside in winter,

And always the warm, soft smile of a friend.

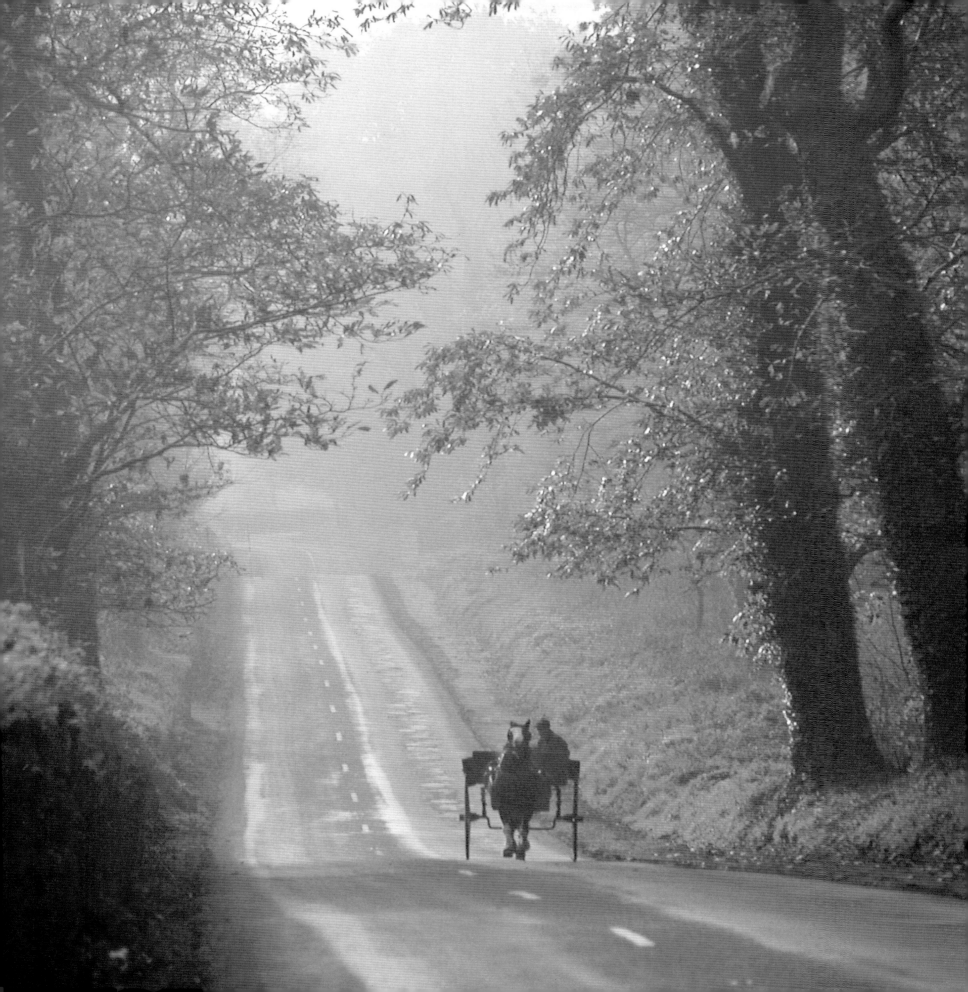

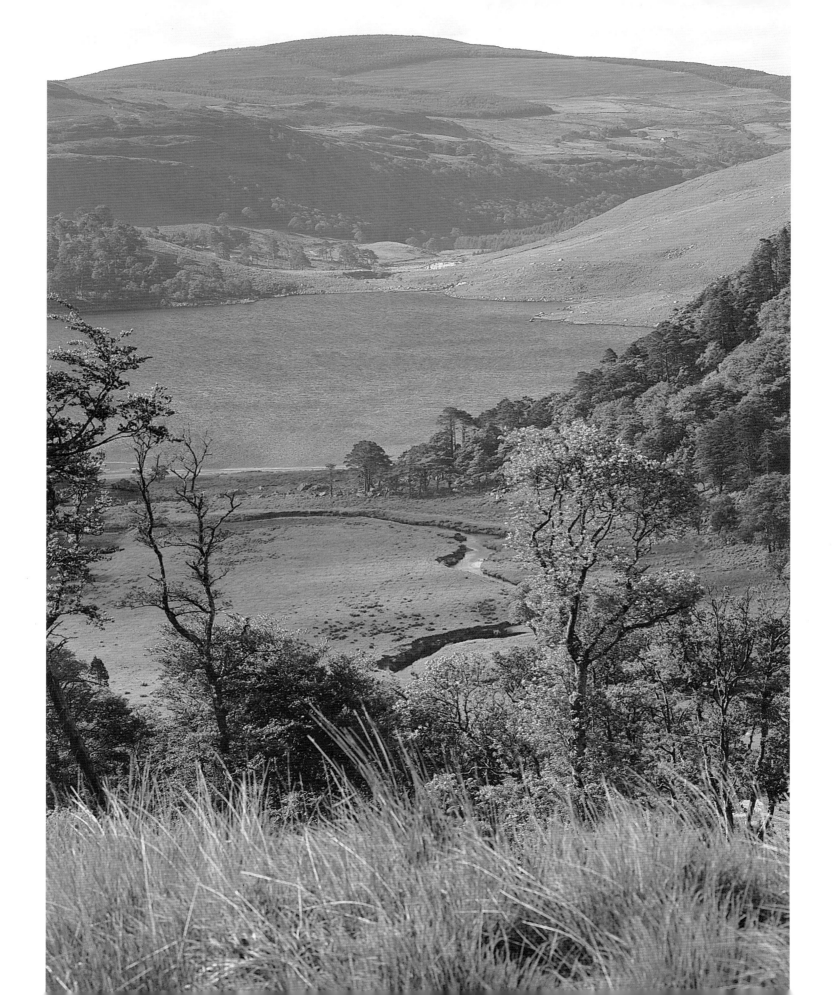

Hills as green as emeralds

Cover the countryside,

    Lakes as blue as sapphires

Are Ireland's special pride,

    And rivers that shine like silver

    Make Ireland look so fair—

But the friendliness of her people

    Is the richest treasure there.

here's a dear little plant that grows in our isle

'Twas Saint Patrick himself sure that set it

And the sun on his labor with pleasure did smile

And a tear from his eyes oft-times wet it

It grows through the bog, through the brake,

    through the mireland

And they call it the dear little Shamrock of Ireland.

TRADITIONAL IRISH FOLK SONG

May the raindrops
    fall lightly on your brow;

              May the soft winds
                freshen your spirit;

          May the sunshine
            brighten your heart;

May the burdens of the day
      rest lightly upon you;

              And may God enfold you
             in the mantle of His love.

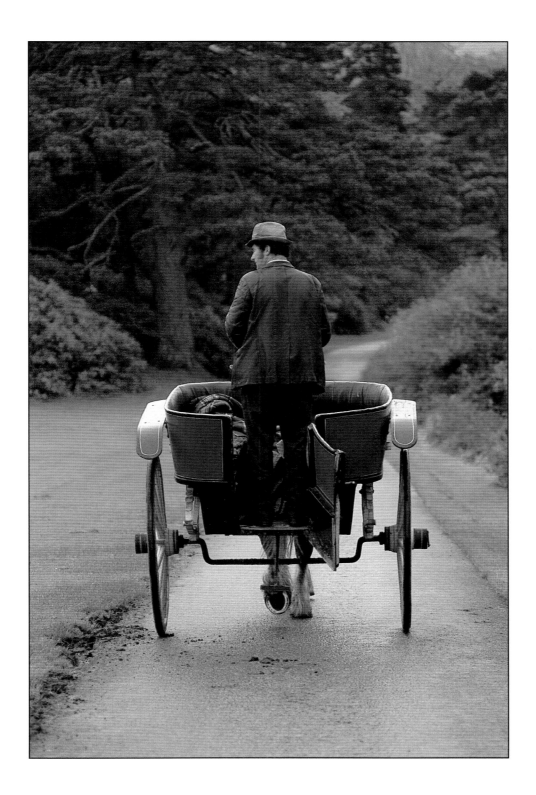

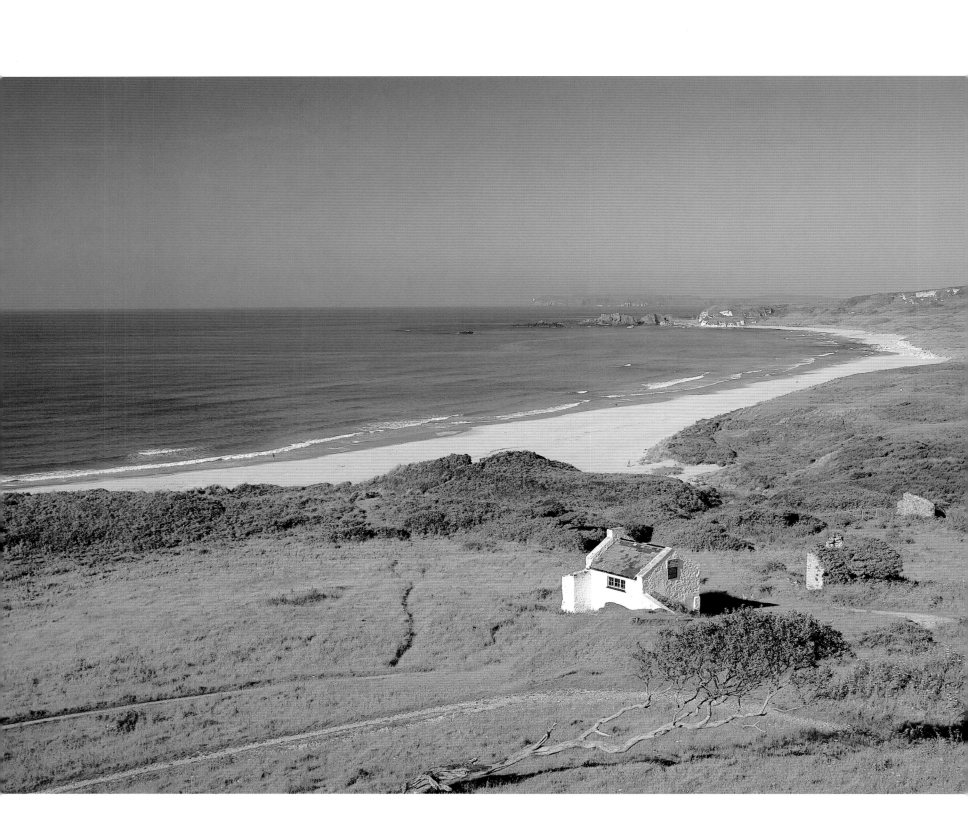

There is not in the wide world a valley so sweet

As that vale in whose bosom the bright waters meet;

Oh! the last rays of feeling and life must depart,

Ere the bloom of that valley shall fade from my heart.

THOMAS MOORE
IRISH SONGWRITER (1779–1852)

No! no land doth rank above thee

Or for loveliness or worth

So shall I, from this day forth,

Ever sing and love thee.

James Clarence Mangan
Irish poet (1803–1849)

I WILL ARISE AND GO NOW, FOR ALWAYS

NIGHT AND DAY

I HEAR LAKE WATER LAPPING WITH LOW

SOUNDS BY THE SHORE;

WHILE I STAND ON THE ROADWAY, OR ON

THE PAVEMENTS GREY,

I HEAR IT IN THE DEEP HEART'S CORE.

W. B. Yeats
Irish writer and statesman (1865–1939)

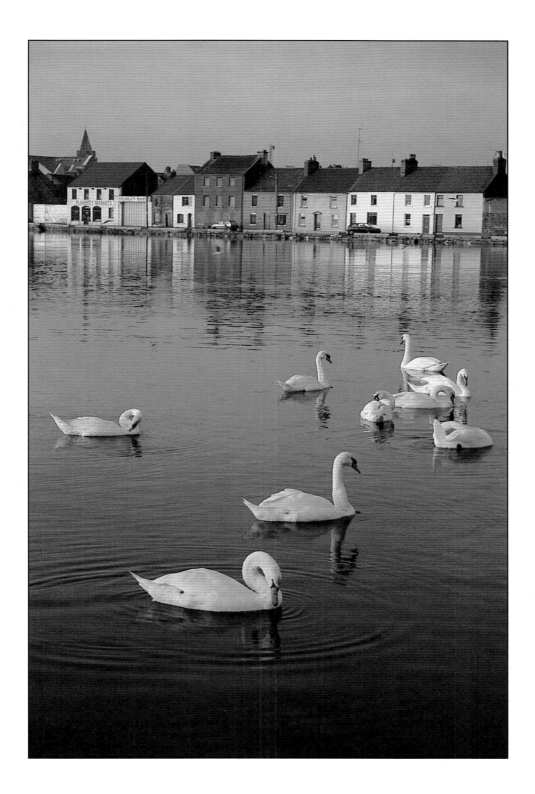

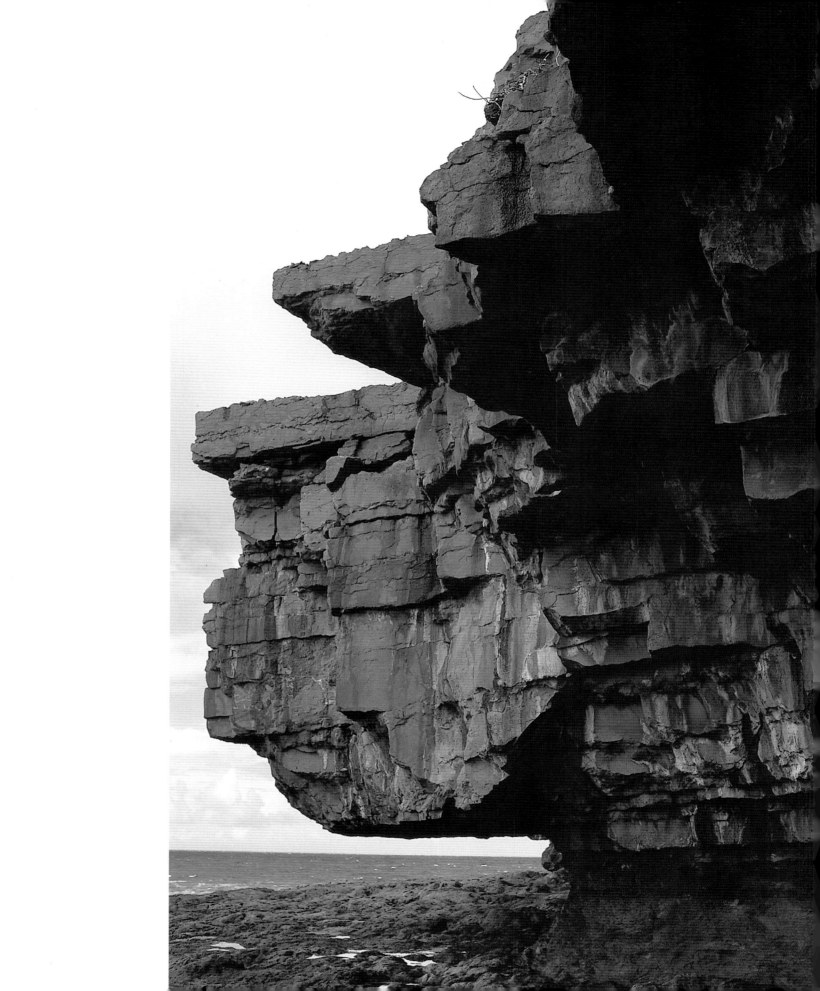

O dim delicious heaven of dreams—

    The land of boyhood's dewey glow—

Again I hear your torrent streams

    Through purple gorge and valley flow,

    Whilst fresh the mountain breezes blow.

Above the air smites sharp and clear—

    The silent lucid spring it chills

But underneath, move warm amidst

    The bases of the hills.

JOHN O'DONNELL
IRISH POET (1837–1874)

GOD . . . MADE YOU ALL FAIR

YOU IN PURPLE AND GOLD

YOU IN SILVER AND GREEN

'TIL NO EYE THAT HAS SEEN

WITHOUT LOVE CAN BEHOLD.

Dora Sigerson
Irish poet (1866–1918)

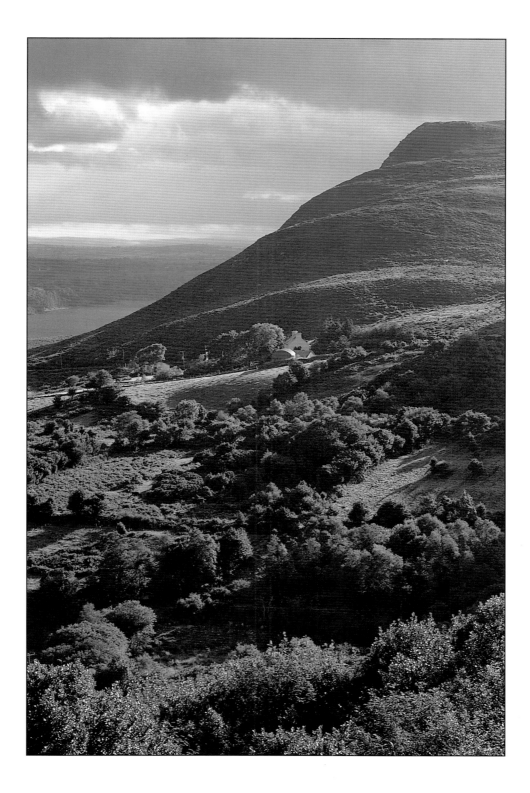

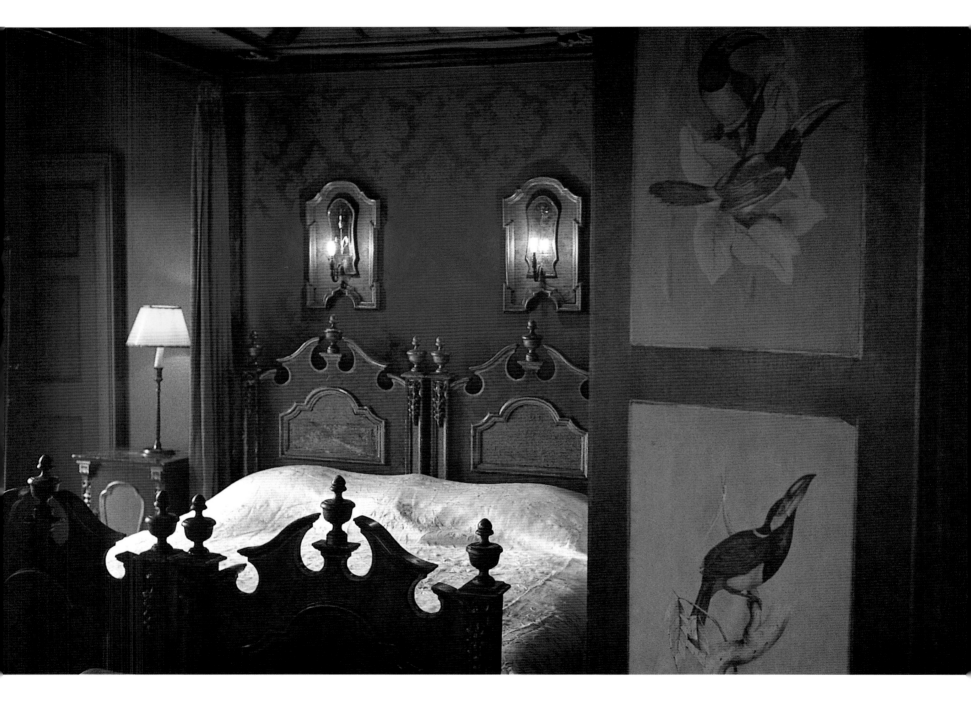

Blessings for the
Home and Hearth

If ever I'm a money'd man, I mean, please God, to cast

My golden anchor in the place where youthful years were pass'd

Though heads that bow are black and brown must meanwhile gather grey

New faces rise by every hearth, and old ones drop away—

Yet dearer still that Irish hill than all the world beside;

It's home, sweet home, where'er I roam, through lands and waters wide.

And if the Lord allows me, I surely will return

To my native Ballyshannon, and the winding banks of Erne.

William Allingham
Irish poet (1824–1889)

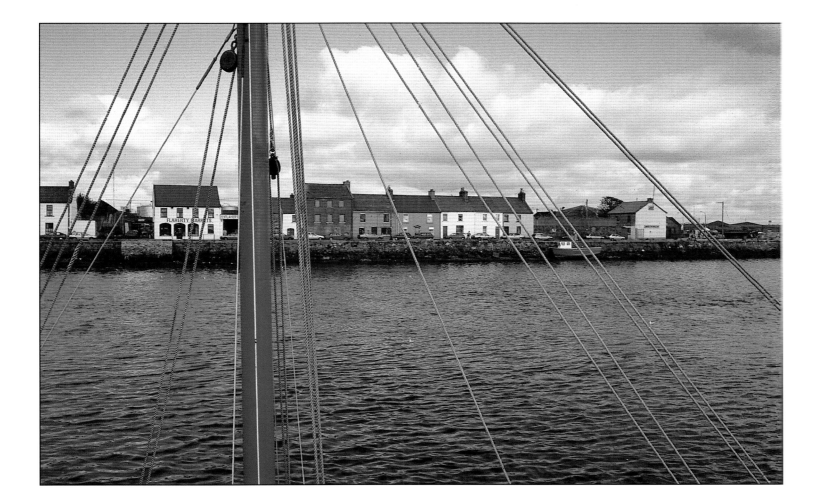

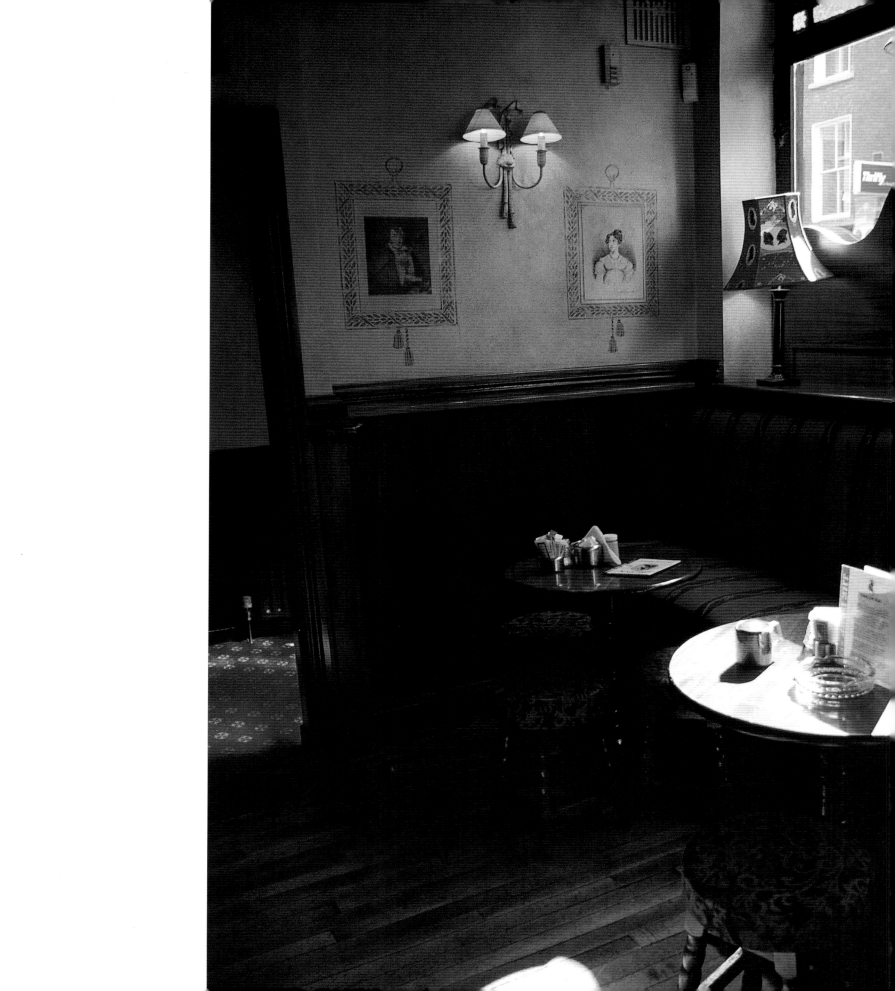

May your glass be ever full.

May the roof over your head be always strong.

And may you be in heaven half an hour

Before the Devil knows you're dead.

May there always be work for your hands to do,

May your purse always hold a coin or two.

May the sun always shine warm on your windowpane,

May a rainbow be certain to follow each rain.

May the hand of a friend always be near you,

And may God fill your heart with gladness to cheer you.

May you live as long as you want,

And never want as long as you live.

Health and a long life to you.

Land without rent to you.

A child every year to you.

And if you can't go to heaven,

May you at least die in Ireland.

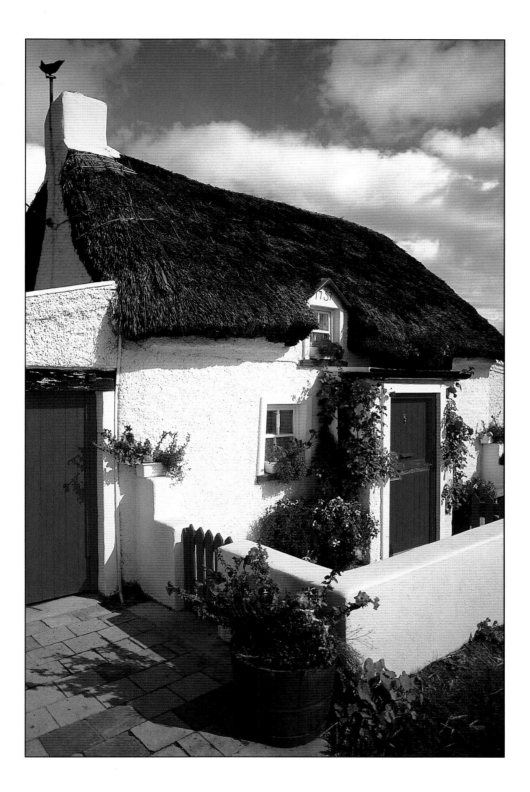

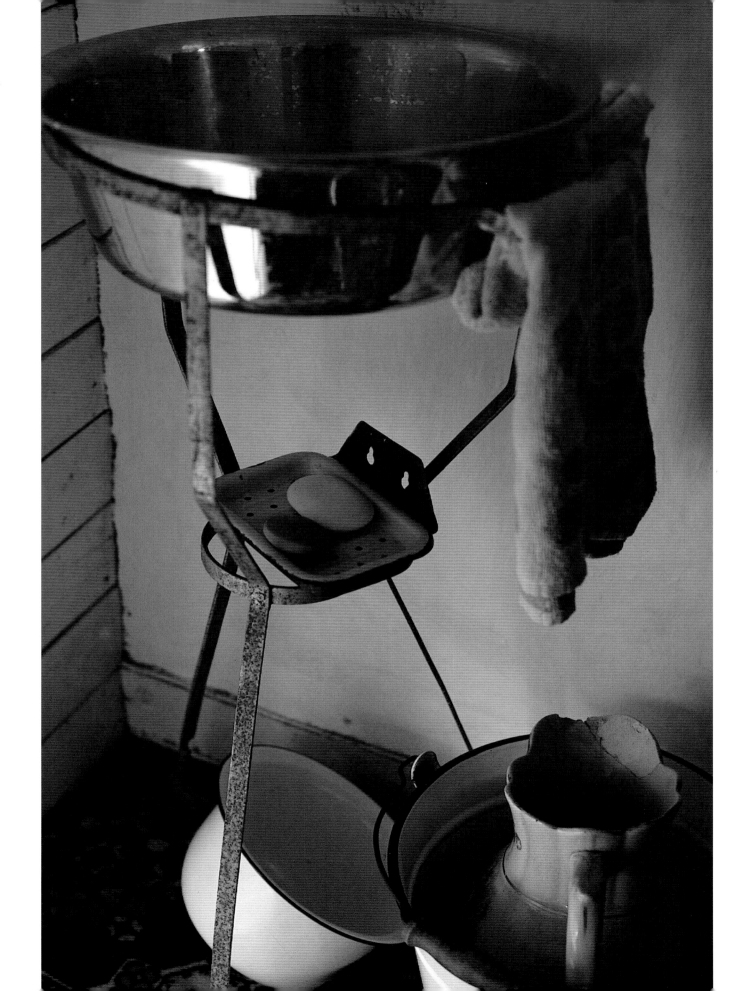

ay you live long,

Die happy,

And rate a mansion in heaven.

May your troubles be less

And your blessings be more.

And nothing but happiness

Come through your door.

May you be poor

      in misfortune,

Rich in blessings,

Slow to make enemies,

And quick to make friends.

But rich or poor,

      quick or slow,

May you know nothing

      but happiness

From this day forward.

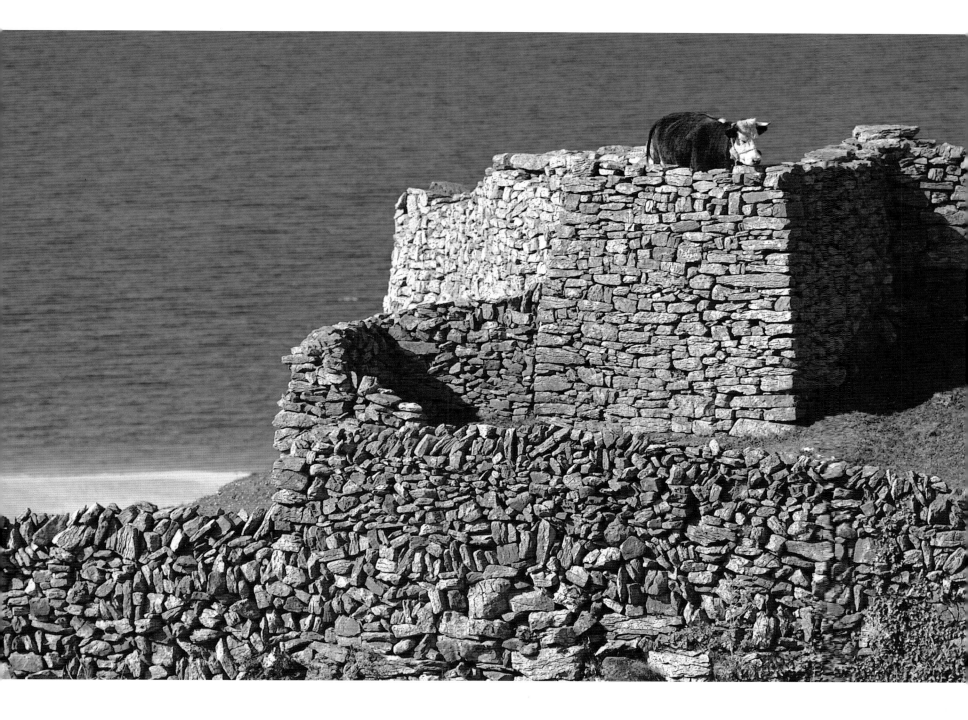

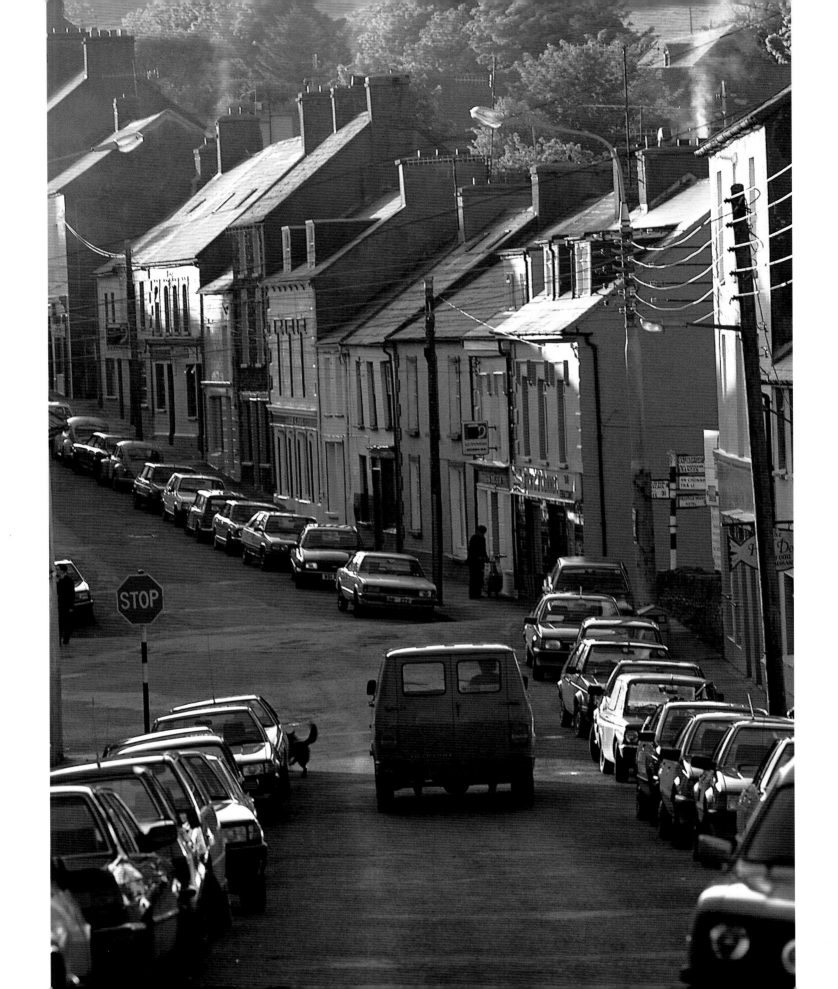

May you have food and raiment,

A soft pillow for your head;

May you be forty years in heaven

Before the devil knows you're dead.

MAY YOUR RIGHT HAND ALWAYS

BE STRETCHED OUT IN FRIENDSHIP

AND NEVER IN WANT.

ay the roof above us never fall in,

And may the friends gathered below it never fall out.

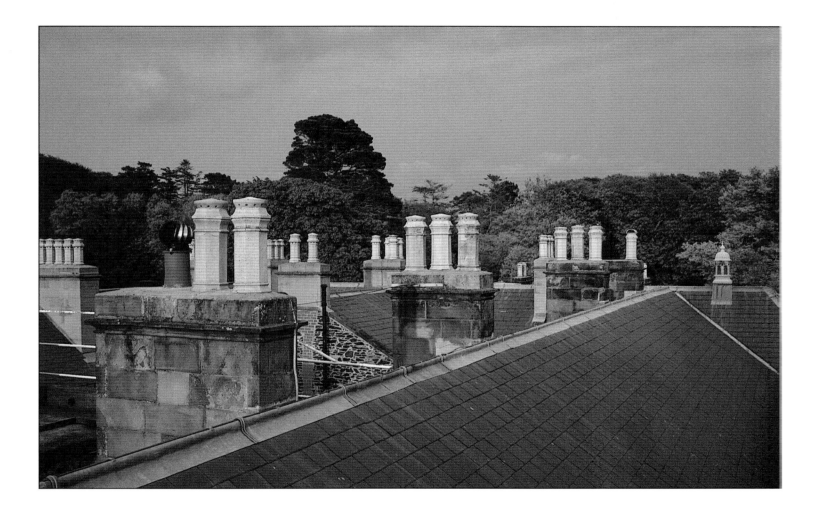

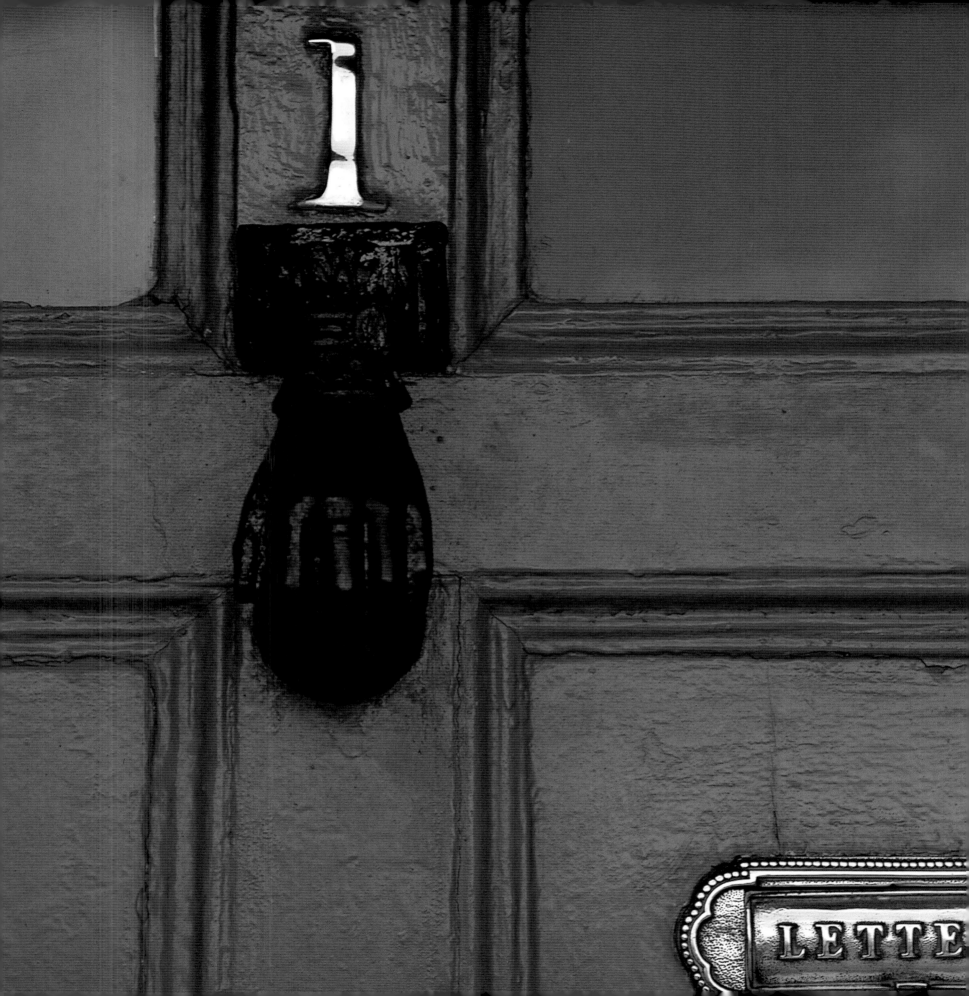

May your neighbors respect you,

Trouble neglect you,

The angels protect you,

And heaven accept you.

MAY THERE BE A GENERATION OF CHILDREN

ON THE CHILDREN OF YOUR CHILDREN.

Bless you and yours

As well as the cottage you live in.

May the roof overhead be well thatched

And those inside be well matched.

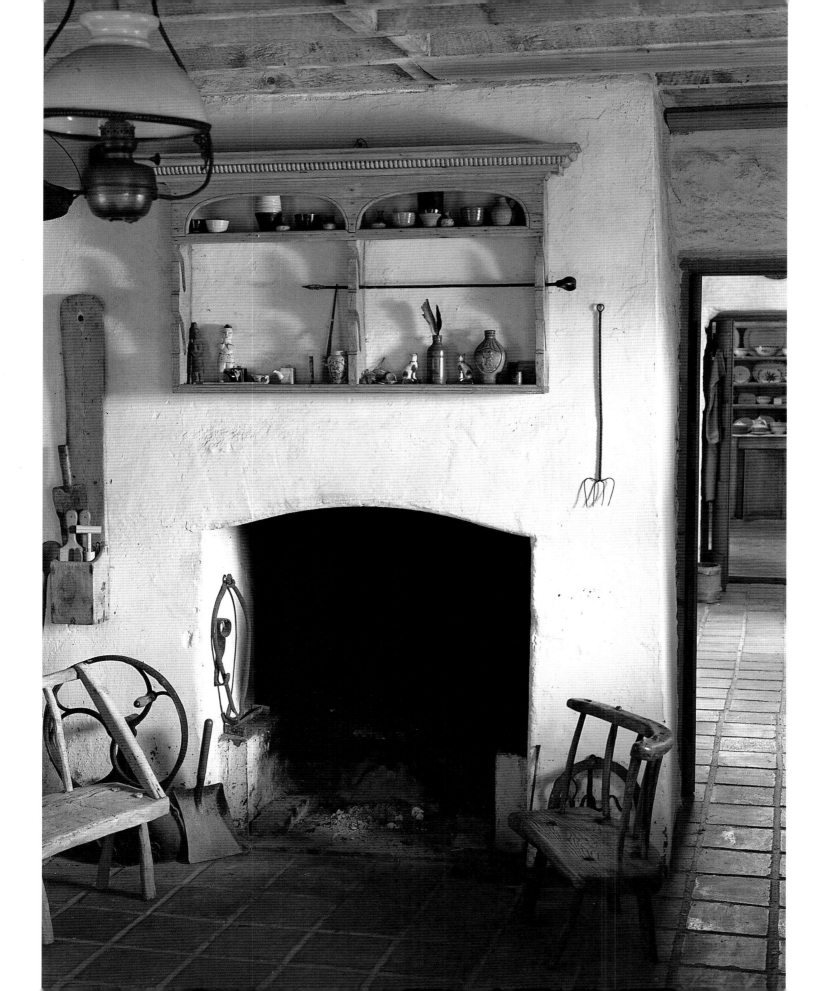

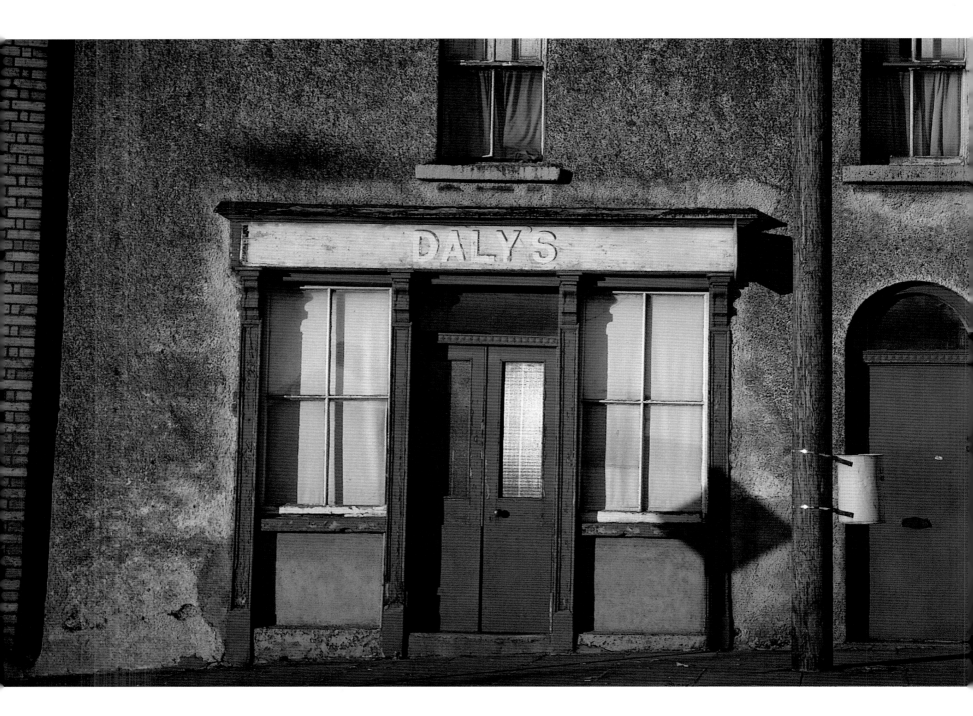

MAY JOY AND PEACE SURROUND YOU,

CONTENTMENT LATCH YOUR DOOR,

AND HAPPINESS BE WITH YOU NOW

AND BLESS YOU EVERMORE.

A Blessing for You and Yours

MAY THE GRACE OF GOD'S PROTECTION

AND HIS GREAT LOVE ABIDE

WITHIN YOUR HOME AND WITHIN THE HEARTS

OF ALL WHO DWELL INSIDE.

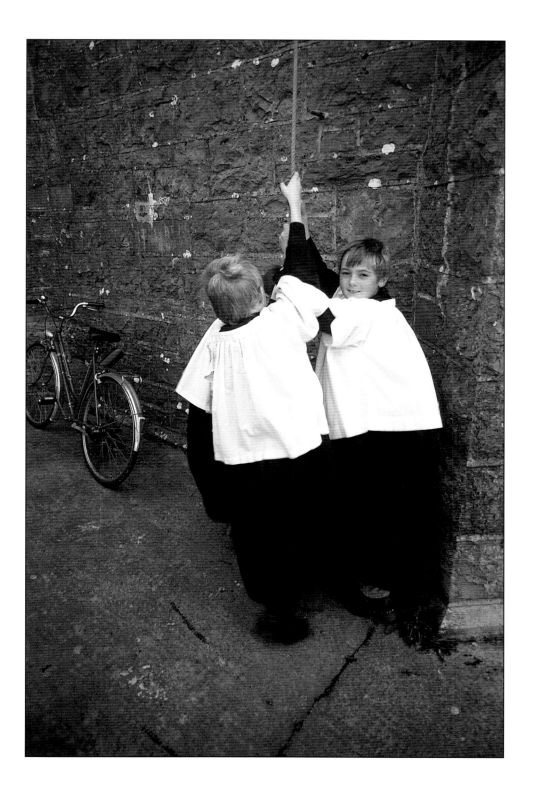

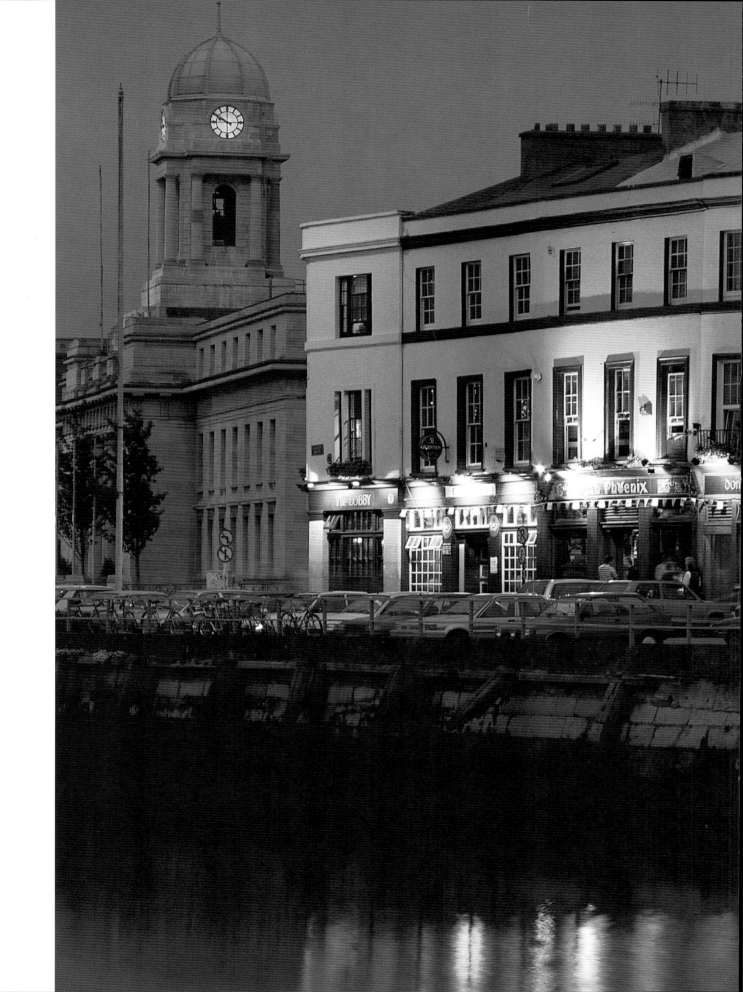

May your home be filled with laughter,

May your pockets be filled with gold,

And may you have all the happiness

Your Irish heart can hold.

alls for the wind

And a roof for the rain,

And drinks by the fire.

Laughter to cheer you

And those you love near you

And all that your heart may desire!

Bless the four corners of this house,

And be the lintel blessed.

Bless the hearth,

And bless the board,

And bless each place of rest.

And bless the door that opens to strangers as to kin,

And bless each shining window

That lets the sunlight in.

Bless the oak tree overhead,

Bless every sturdy wall,

And may the peace of God above be always on us all.

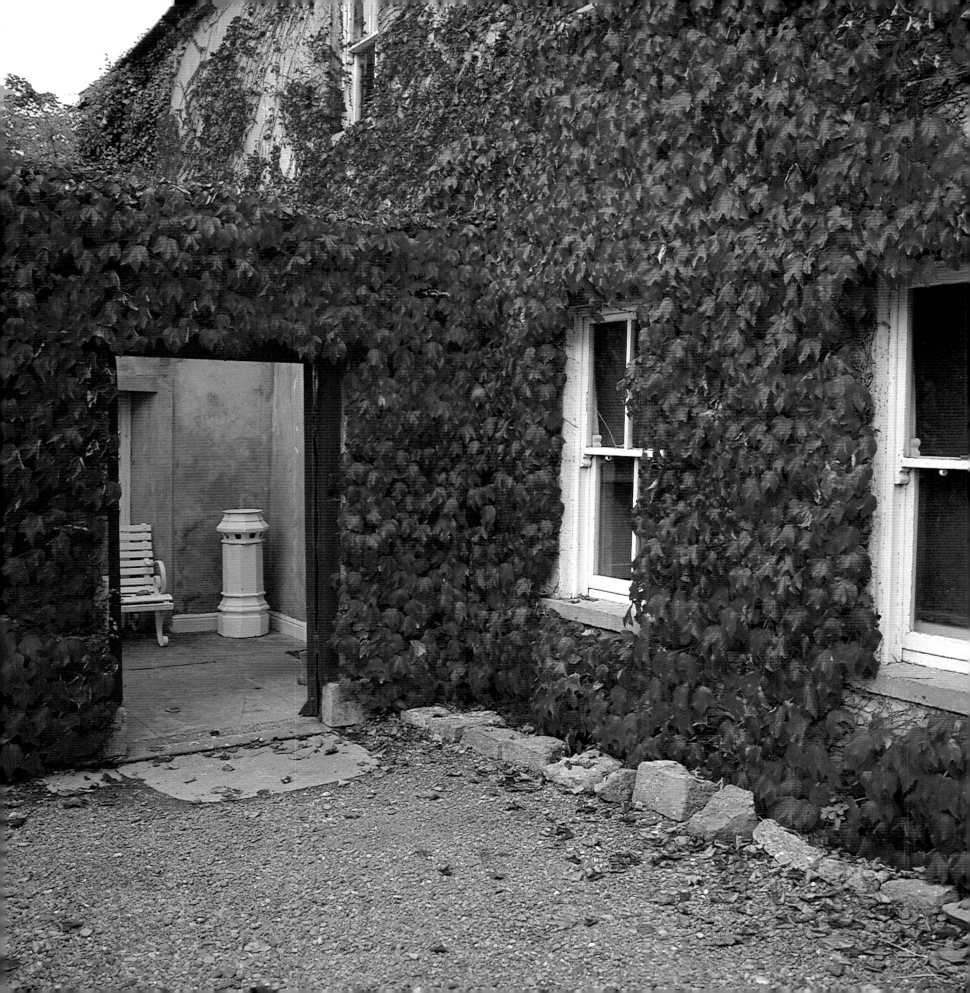

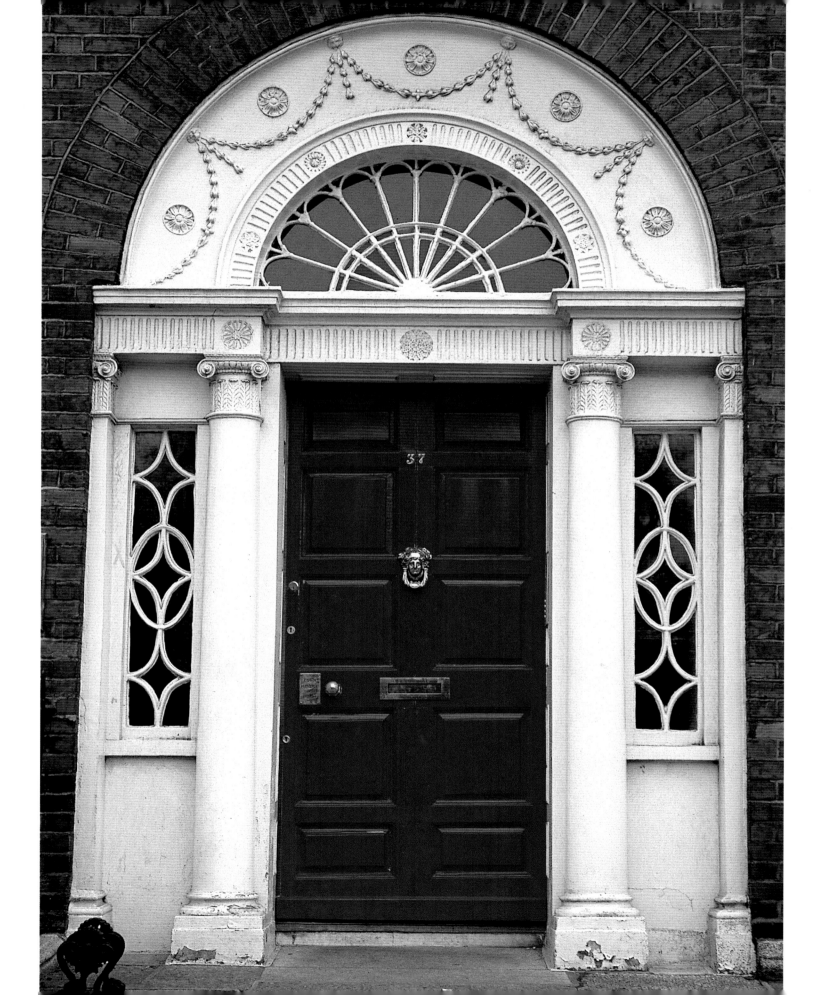

May your home always be too small to hold
all of your friends.

May those who love us, love us.

And those who don't love us,

May God turn their hearts.

And if He doesn't turn their hearts,

May He turn their ankles,

So we may know them by their limping!

Calm be thy sleep as infants' slumbers!

Pure as angel thoughts thy dreams!

May every joy this bright world numbers

Shed o'er thee their mingled beams!

Thomas Moore
Irish songwriter (1779–1852)

In the December weather, grey and grim,

In the December twilight, keen and cold,

Stood the farmhouse on the green-reached hill

Piled with thatched rooves, mellowed into gold . . .

JOHN O'DONNELL
IRISH POET (1837–1874)

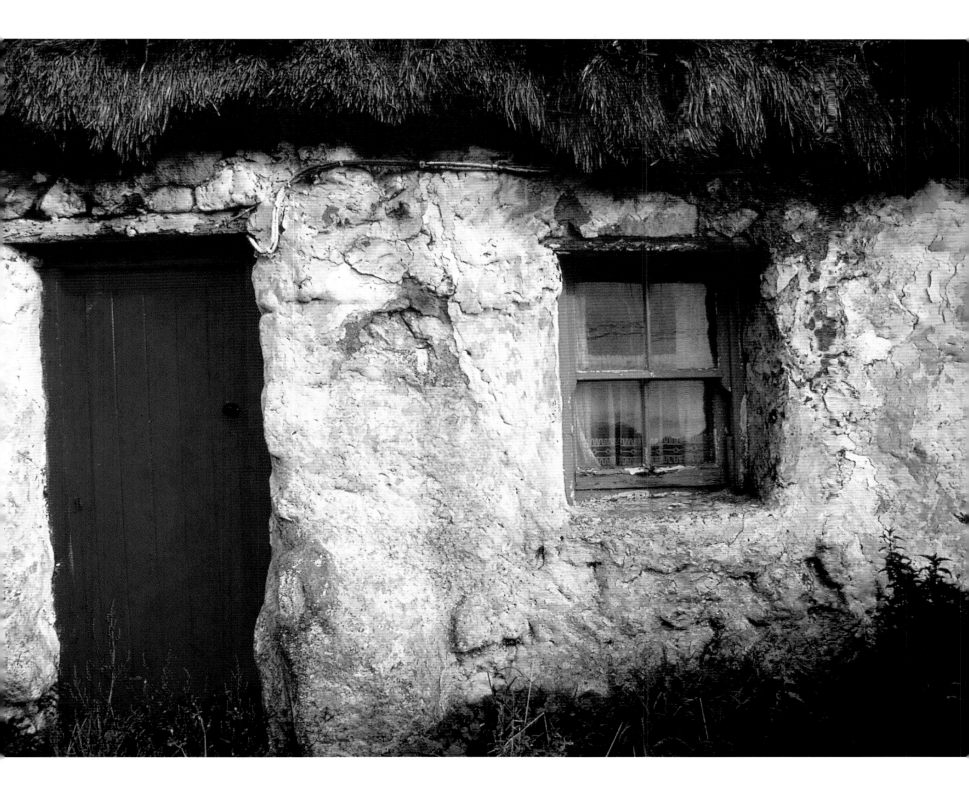

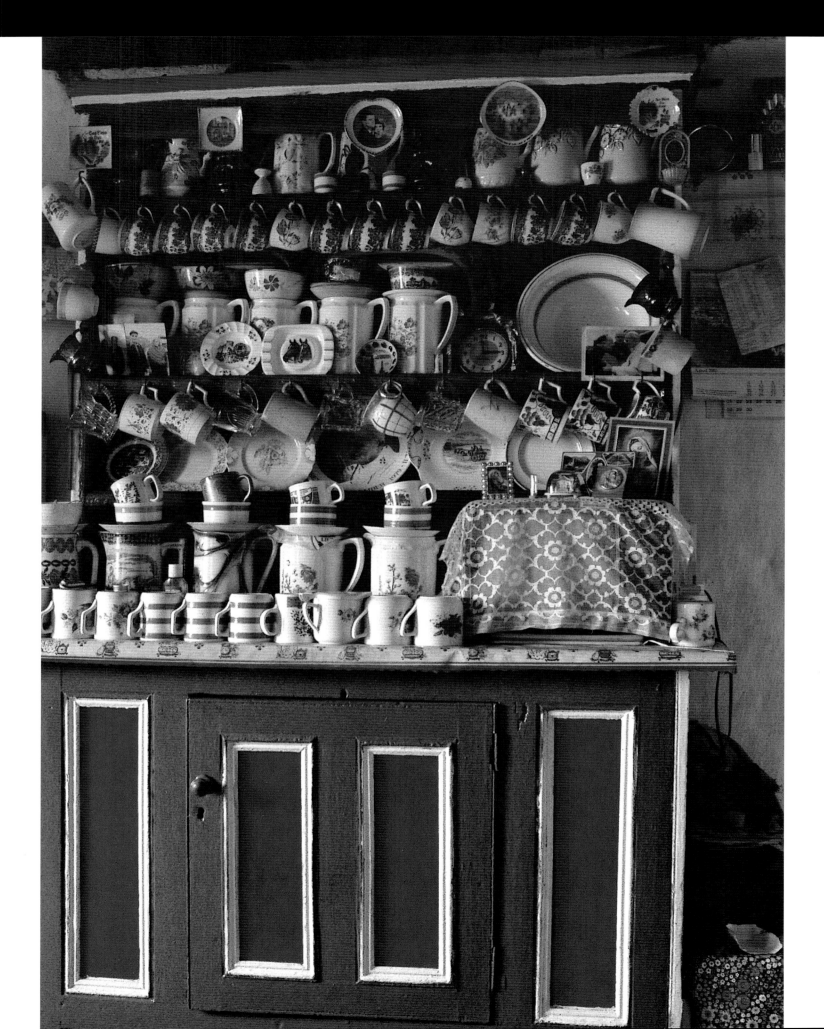

St. Brigid's Blessing

God bless the poor,

God bless the sick,

God bless our human race;

God bless our food,

God bless our drink

And our homes, O God, embrace.

St. Brigid of Kildare
6th-century Irish cleric

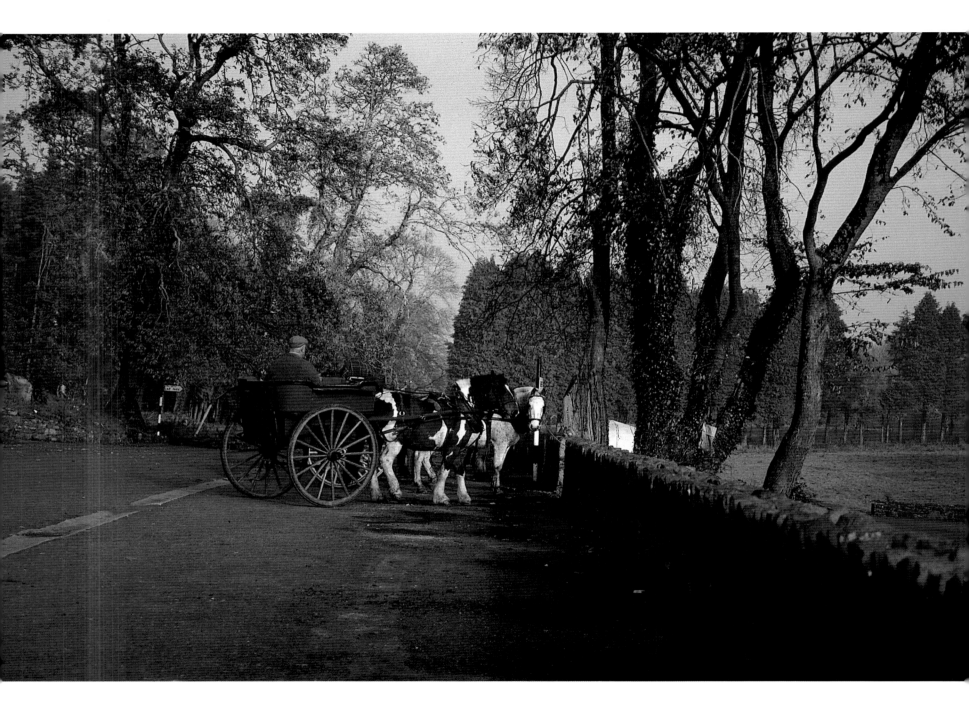

Blessings for the Journey

I've wandered by the rolling Lee!

And Lene's green bowers—

I've seen the Shannon's wide-spread sea,

And Limerick's towers—

And Liffey's tide, where halls of pride

Frown o'er the flood below . . .

Edward Walsh
Irish poet (1805–1850)

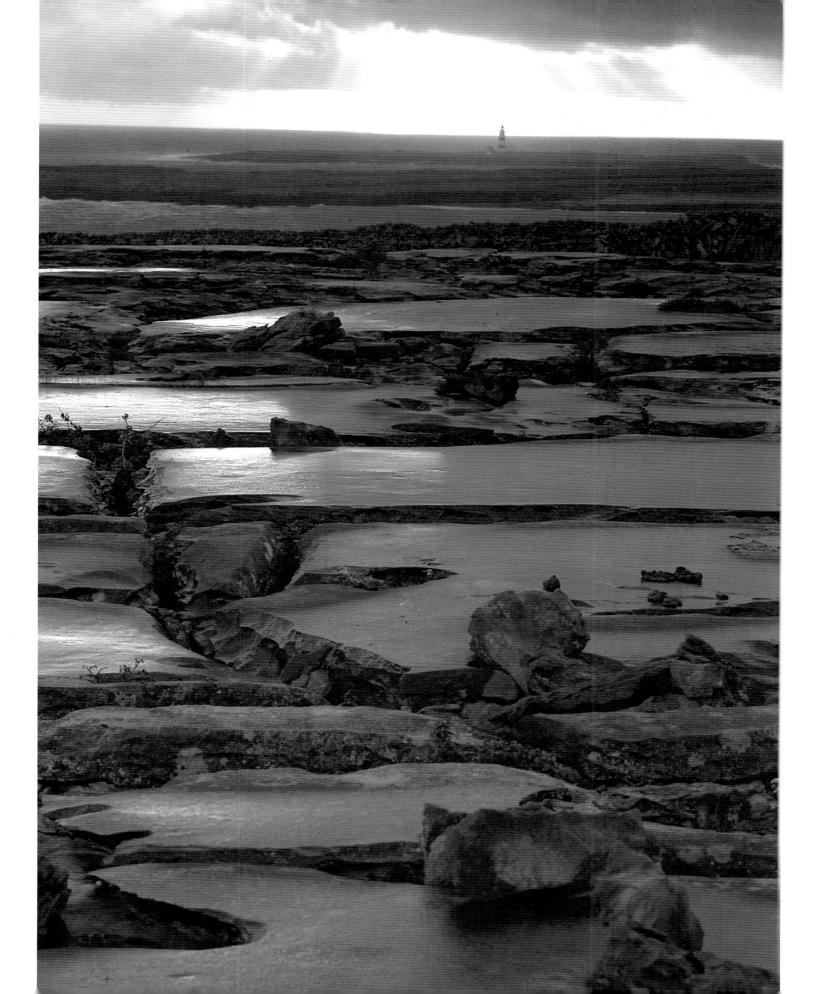

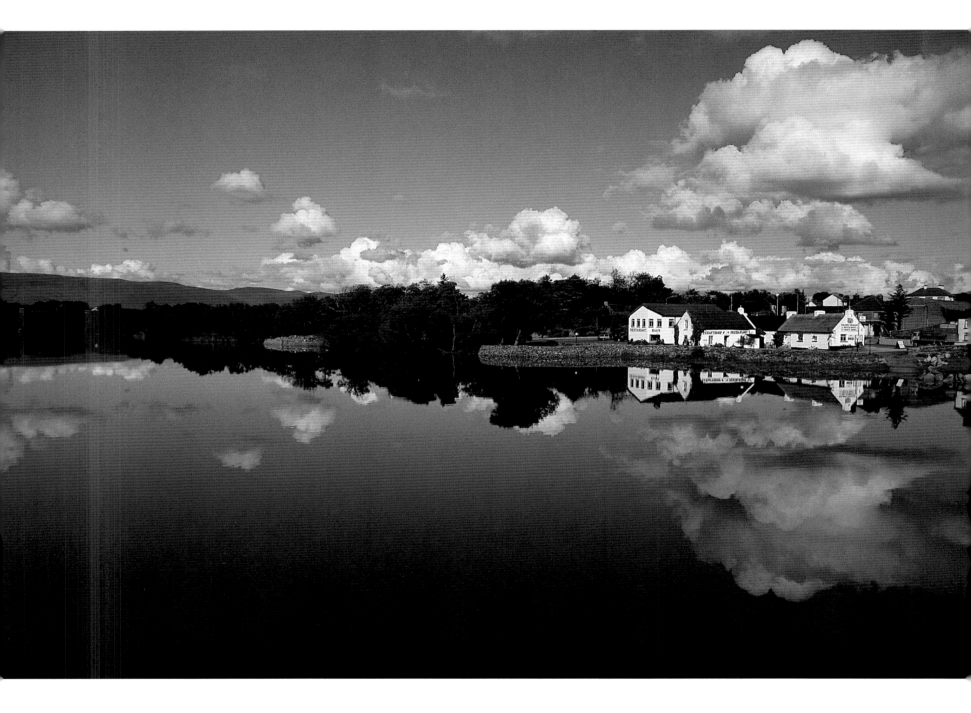

May the leprechauns be near you,

To spread luck along your way.

And may all the Irish angels

Smile on you St. Patrick's Day.

May the blessings of each day

Be the blessings you need most.

MAY THE ROAD RISE TO MEET YOU.

MAY THE WIND BE ALWAYS AT YOUR BACK.

MAY THE SUN SHINE WARM UPON YOUR FACE.

AND RAINS FALL SOFT UPON YOUR FIELDS.

AND UNTIL WE MEET AGAIN,

MAY GOD HOLD YOU IN THE HOLLOW OF HIS HAND.

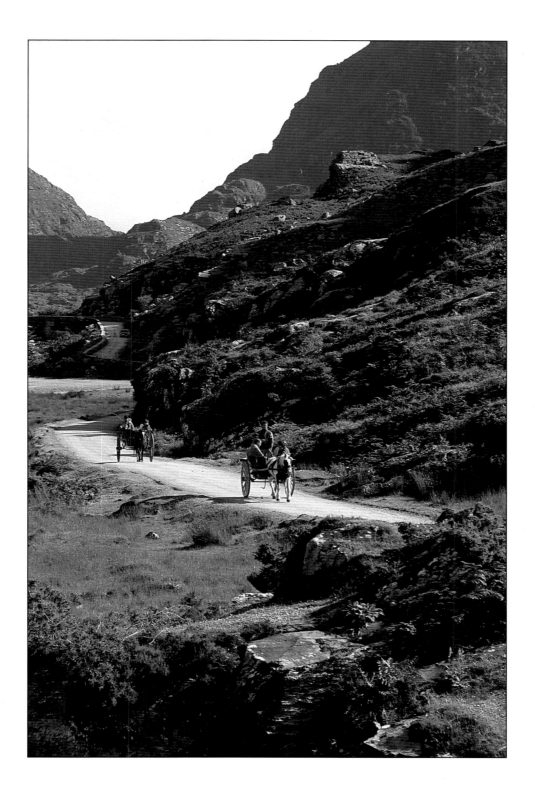

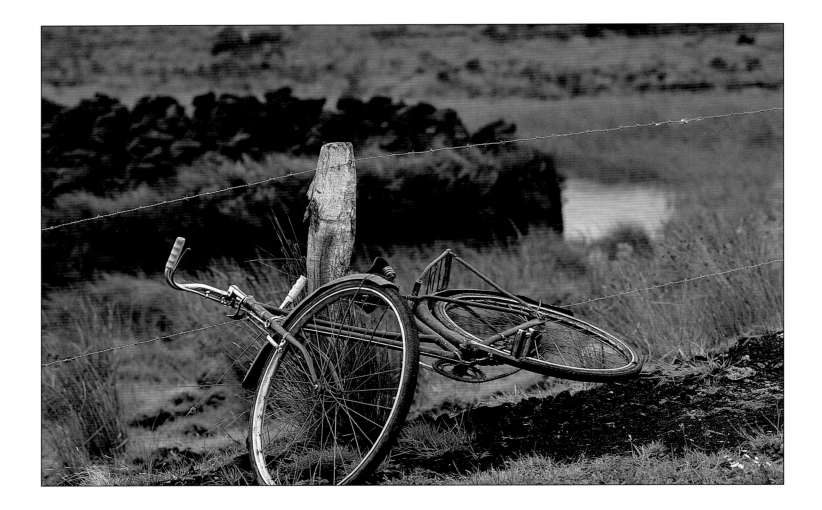

May the blessings of light be upon you,

Light without and light within.

And in all your comings and goings,

May you ever have a kindly greeting

From them you meet along the road.

WHEREVER YOU GO AND WHATEVER YOU DO,

MAY THE LUCK OF THE IRISH BE THERE WITH YOU.

ay you have warm words on a cold evening,

A full moon on a dark night,

And the road downhill all the way to your door.

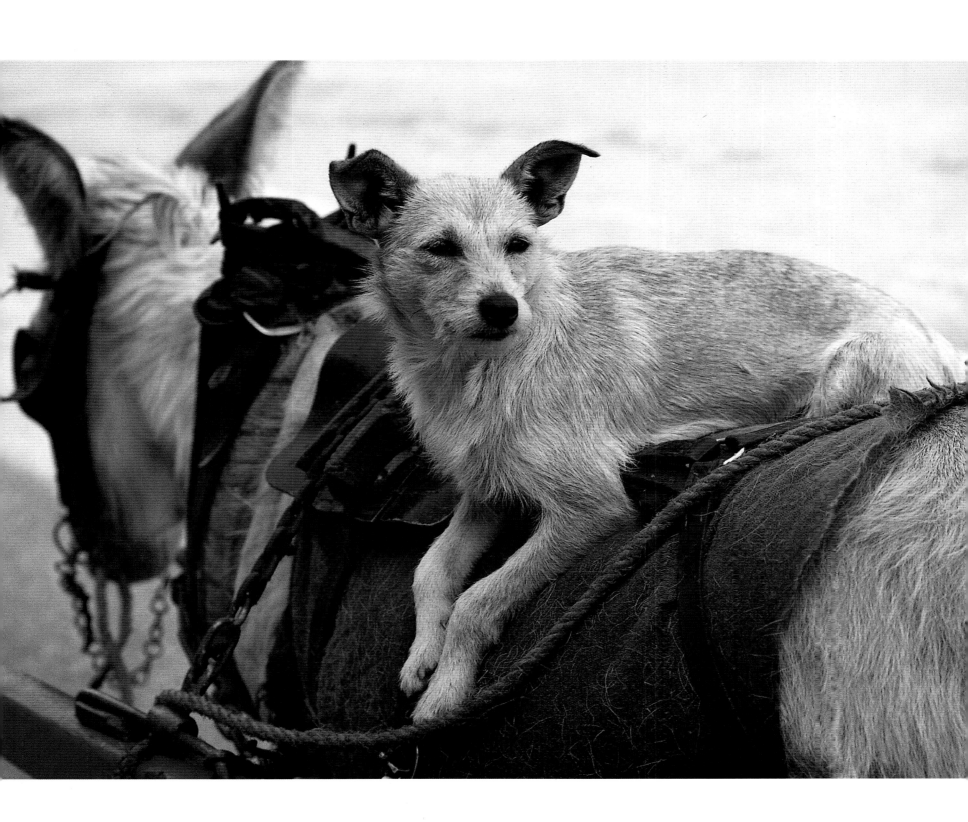

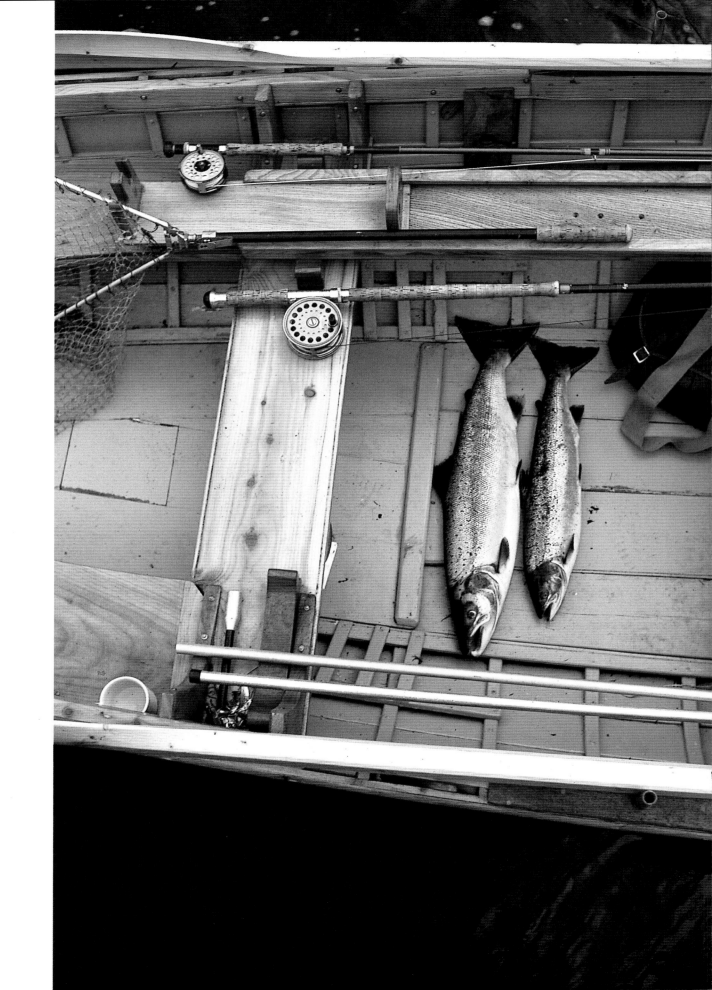

May the good saints protect you

And bless you today

And may troubles ignore you

Each step of the way

MAY GOOD LUCK BE YOUR FRIEND

IN WHATEVER YOU DO,

AND MAY TROUBLE BE ALWAYS

A STRANGER TO YOU.

Lucky stars above you,

Sunshine on your way,

Many friends to love you,

Joy in work and play,

Laughter to outweigh each care,

In your heart a song,

And gladness waiting everywhere

All your whole life long!

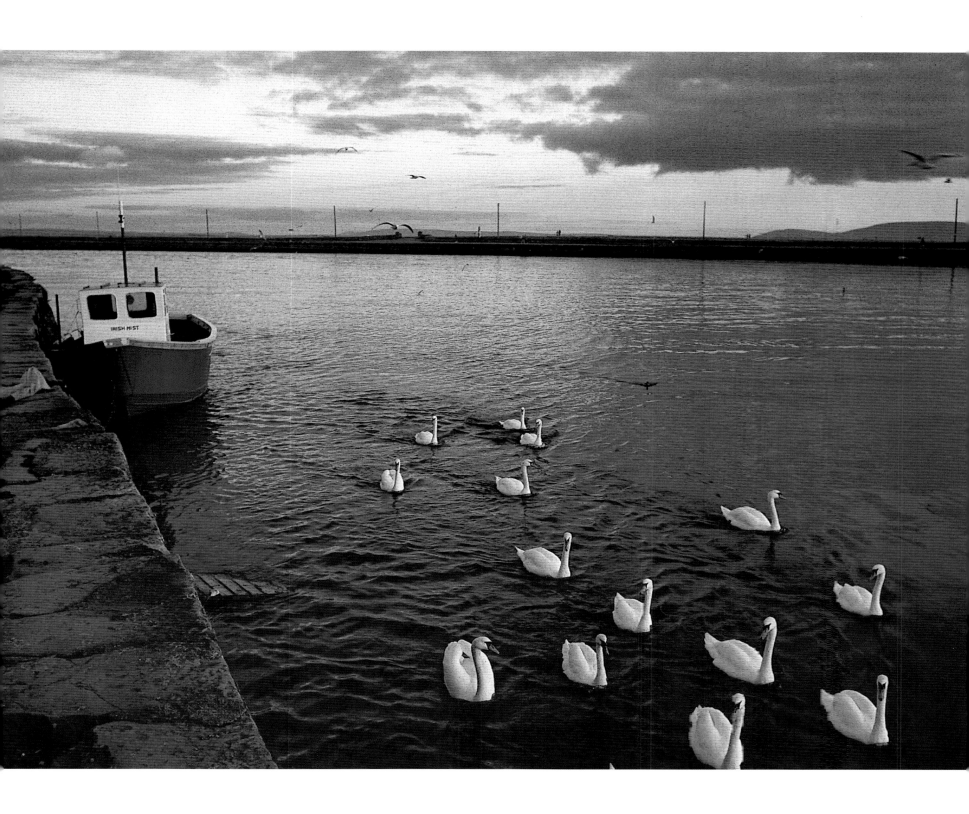

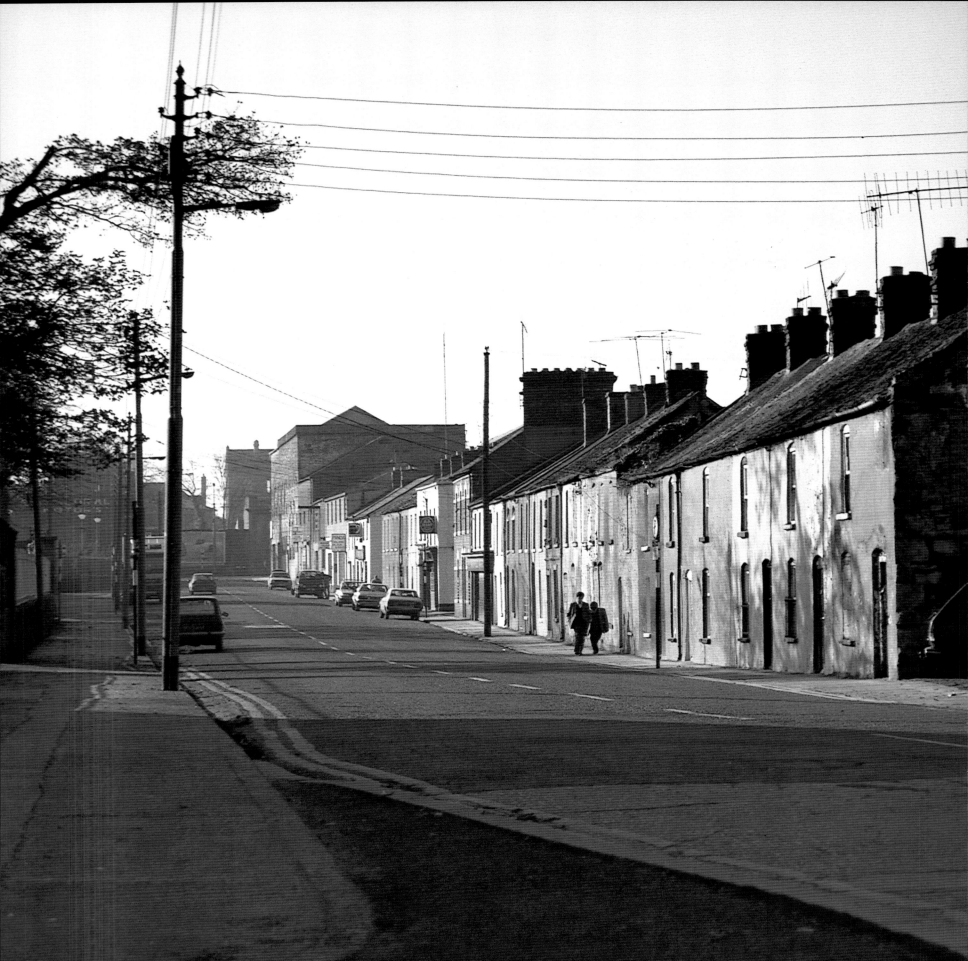

May the lilt of Irish laughter

Lighten every load,

May the mist of Irish magic

Shorten every road,

May you taste the sweetest pleasures

That fortune e're bestowed,

And may all your friends remember

All the favors you are owed.

May the love and protection

Saint Patrick can give

Be yours in abundance

As long as you live.

MAY YOU HAVE ALL THE HAPPINESS

AND LUCK THAT LIFE CAN HOLD—

AND AT THE END OF ALL YOUR RAINBOWS

MAY YOU FIND A POT OF GOLD.

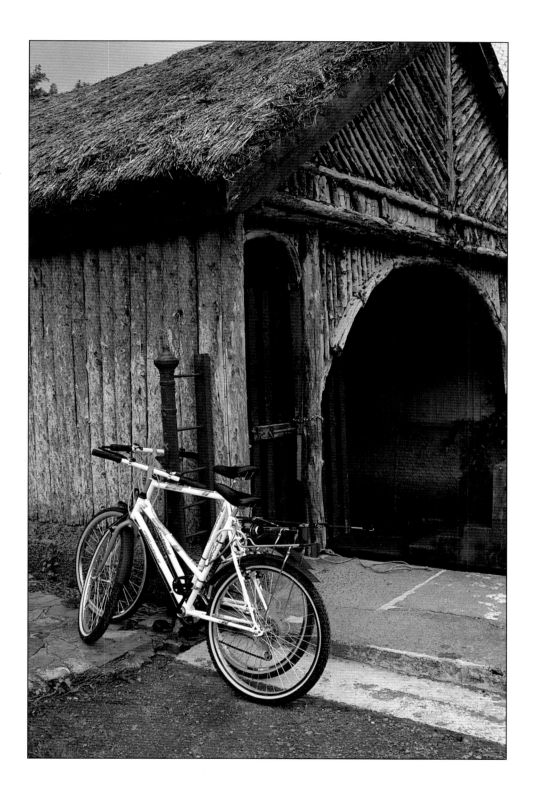

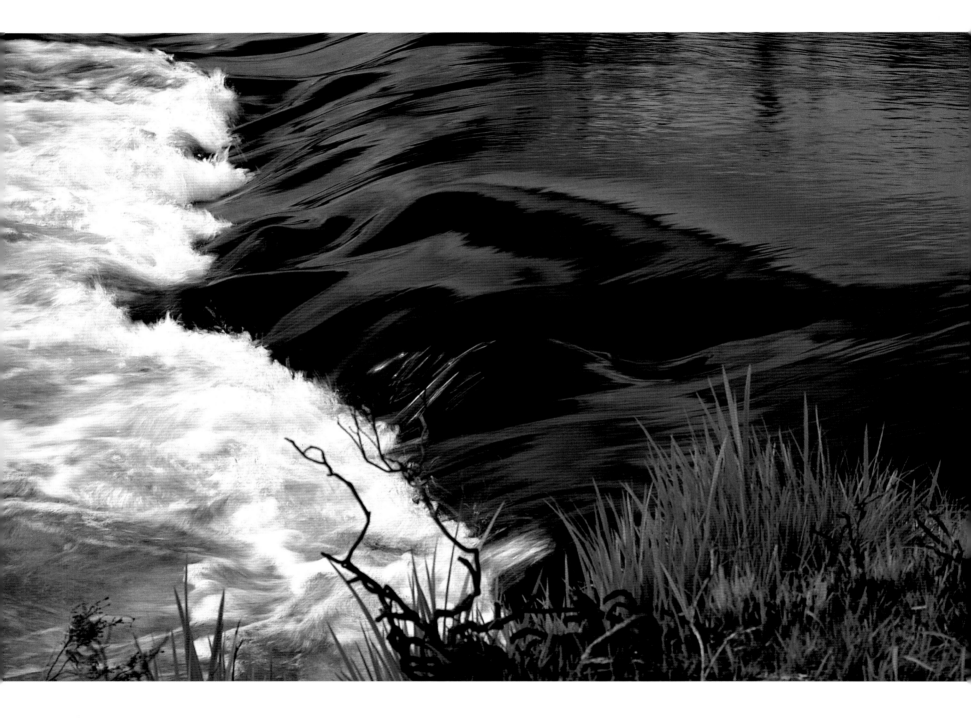

Deep peace of the running waves to you.

Deep peace of the flowing air to you.

Deep peace of the smiling stars to you.

Deep peace of the quiet earth to you.

Deep peace of the watching shepherds to you.

Deep peace of the Son of Peace to you.

May St. Patrick guard you

wherever

You go and guide you in

Whatever you do—

and may his loving

Protection be a blessing

to you always.

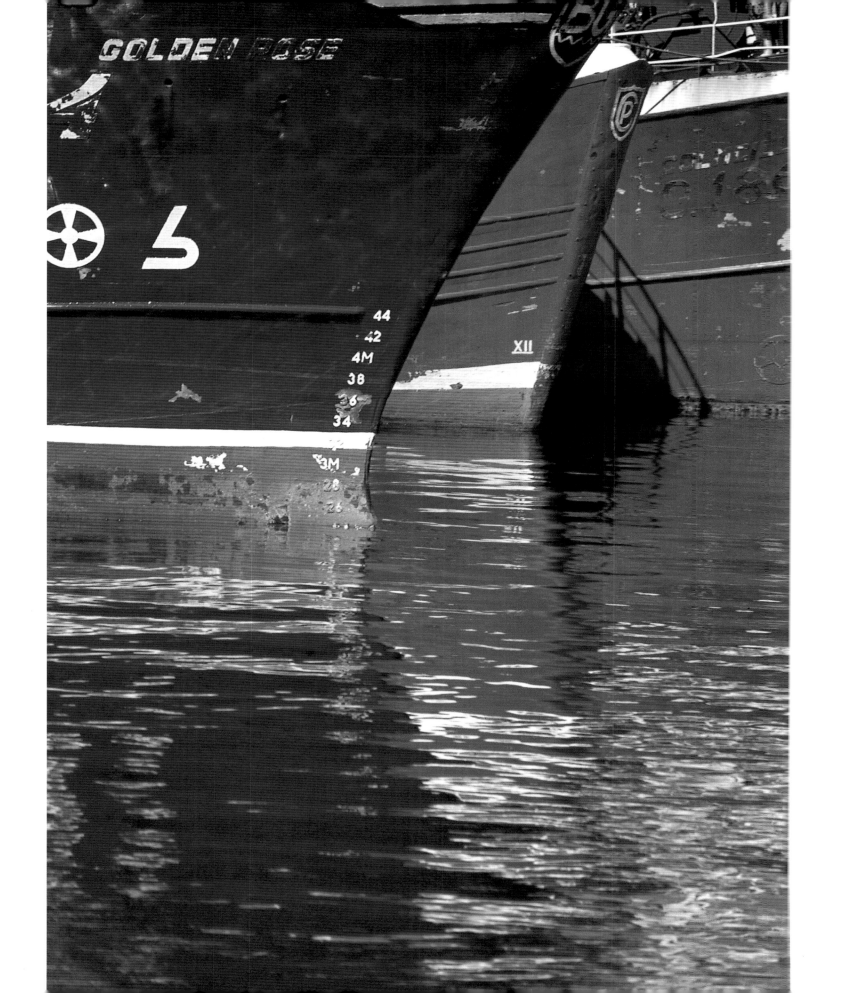

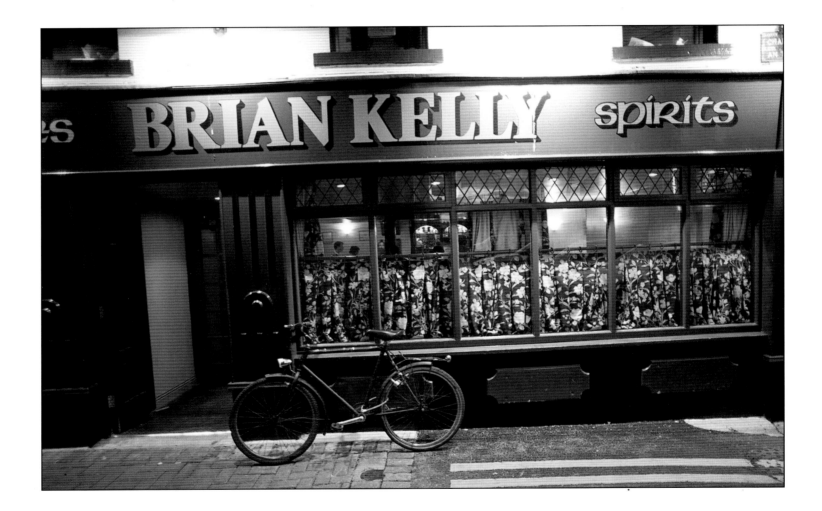

MAY YOU HAVE THE HINDSIGHT TO KNOW WHERE YOU'VE BEEN

THE FORESIGHT TO KNOW WHERE YOU'RE GOING

AND THE INSIGHT TO KNOW WHEN YOU'RE GOING TOO FAR

May you always have a clean shirt,

a clean conscience, and a guinea in your pocket!

May the luck of the Irish possess you;

May the Devil fly off with your worries;

May God bless you forever and ever.

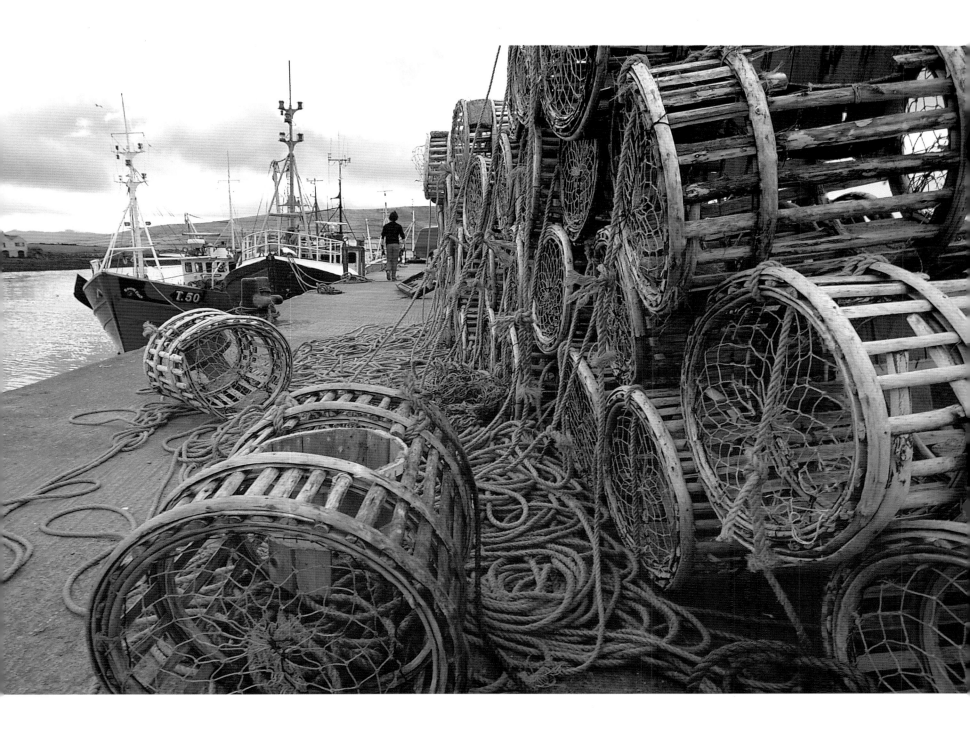

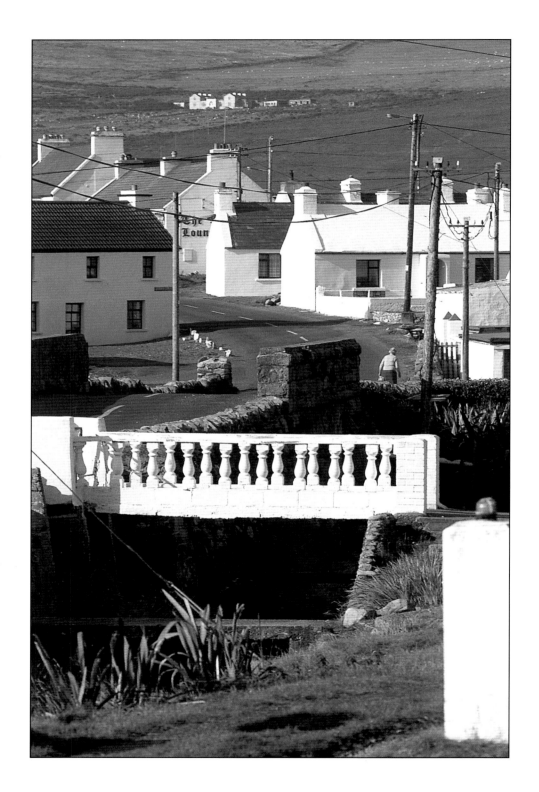

Throughout my journey I did not meet

Another country like the land of O'Neill;

The variegated hillsides bright with dew

The sunny smooth meadows crossed by roads.

Pádraigín Haicéad
17th-century Irish poet

AY THE GOOD LORD TAKE A LIKING TO YOU,

. . . BUT NOT TOO SOON!

It's easy to be pleasant

When life flows by like a song.

But the man worthwhile is the one who can smile

When everything goes dead wrong.

For the test of the heart is trouble,

And it always comes with years.

And the smile that is worth the praises of earth

Is the smile that shines through the tears.

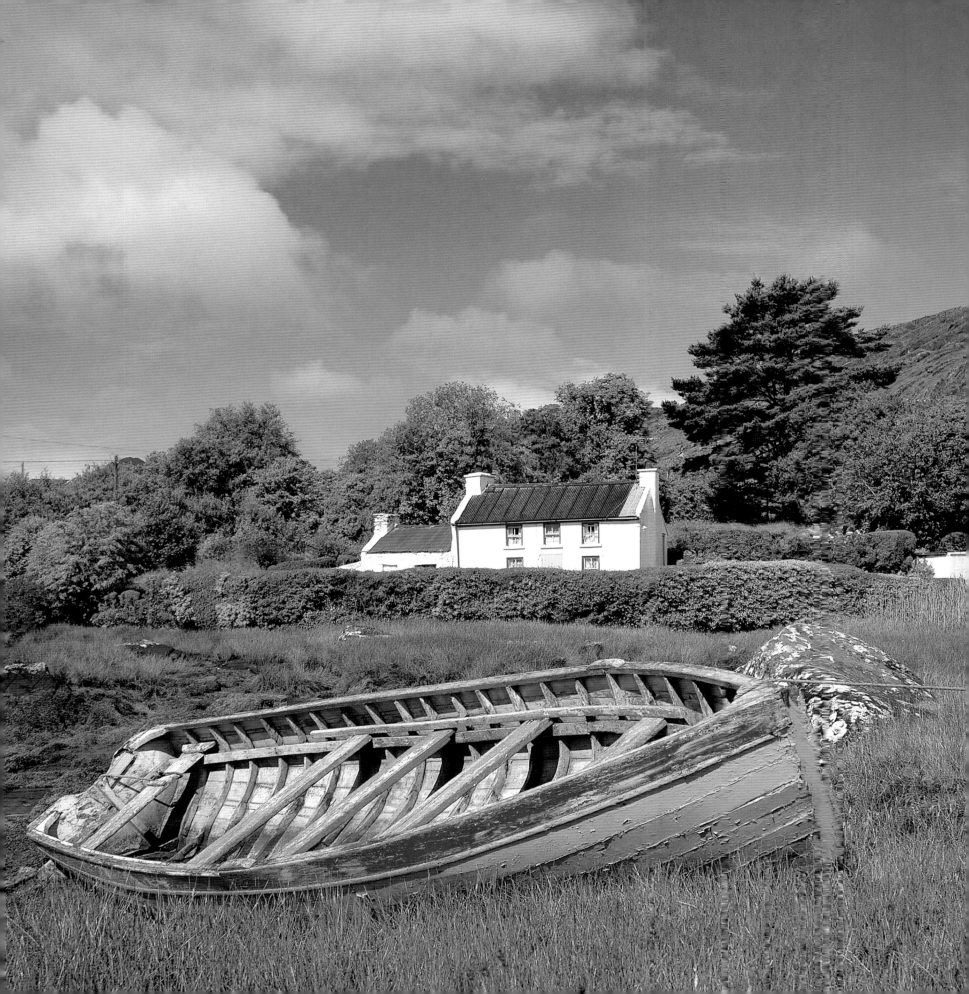

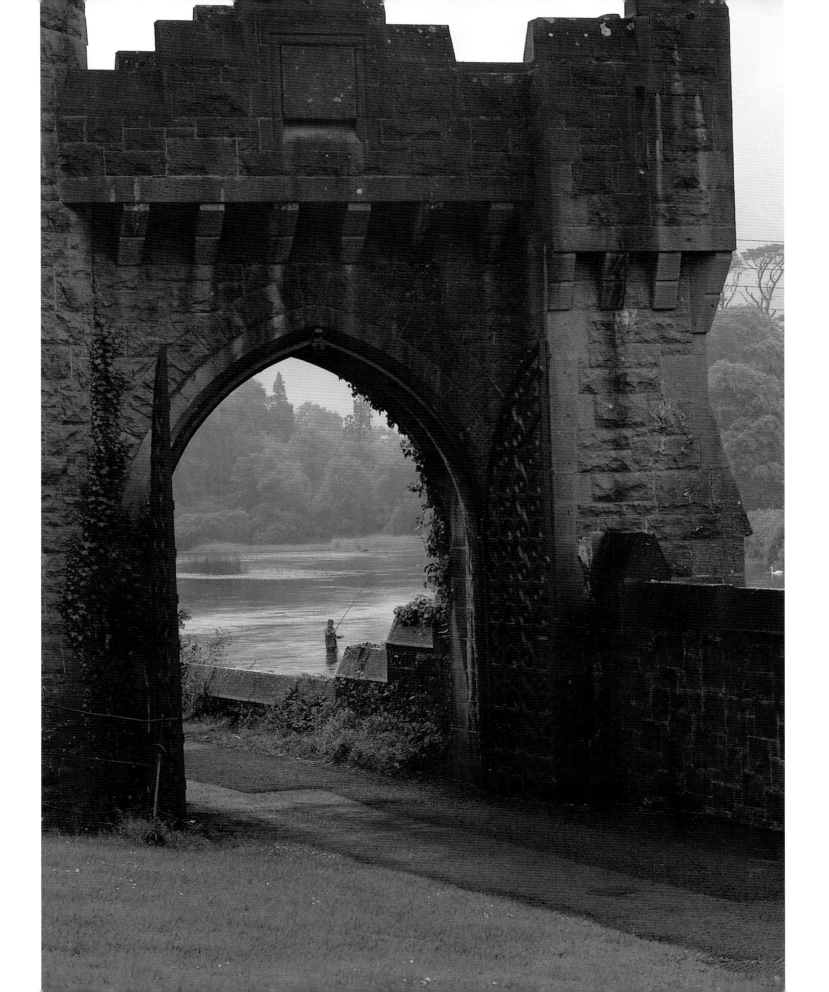

May the joys of today

Be those of tomorrow

And the goblets of life

Hold no dregs of sorrow.

MAY THE SADDEST DAY OF YOUR FUTURE BE NO WORSE

THAN THE HAPPIEST DAY OF YOUR PAST.

May the most you wish for

Be the least you get.

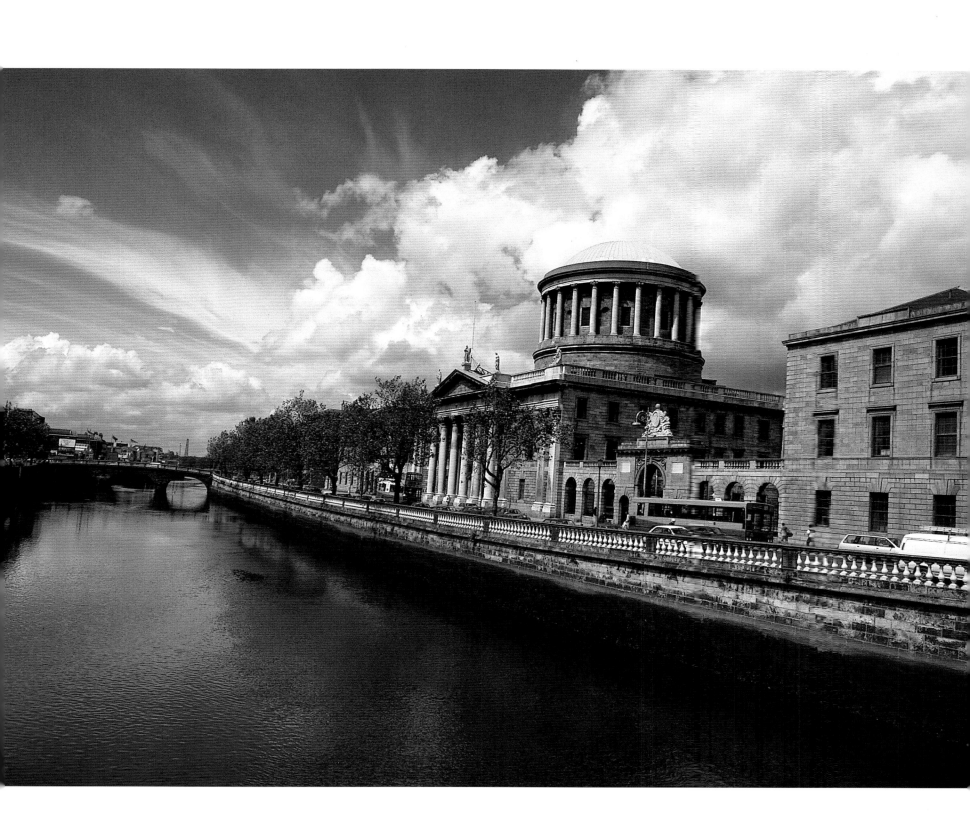

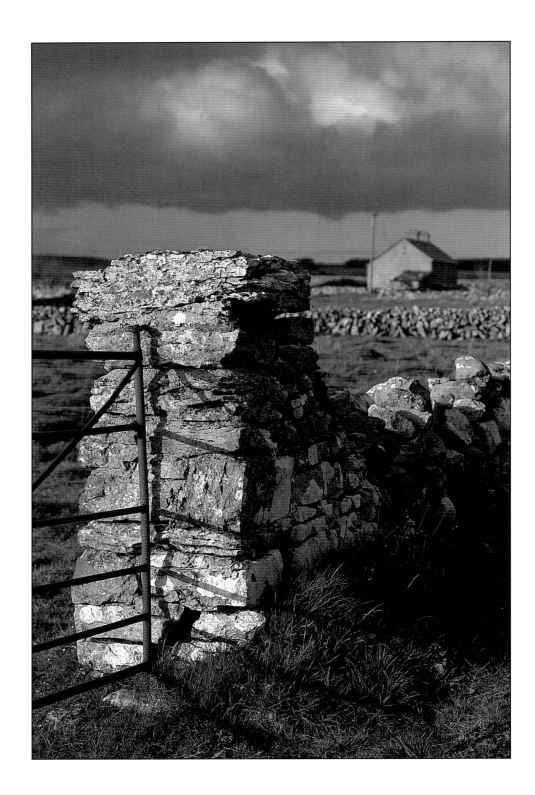

May you have . . .

a song in your heart,

a smile on your lips

and nothing but joy

at your fingertips

May the face of every good news and the back of every bad news be toward us.

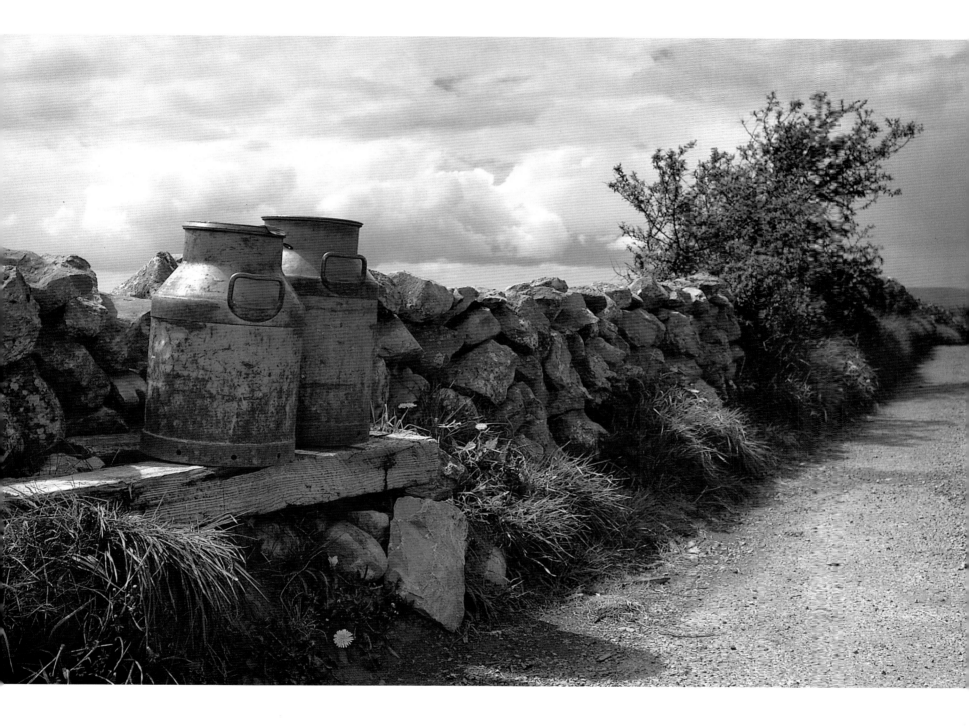

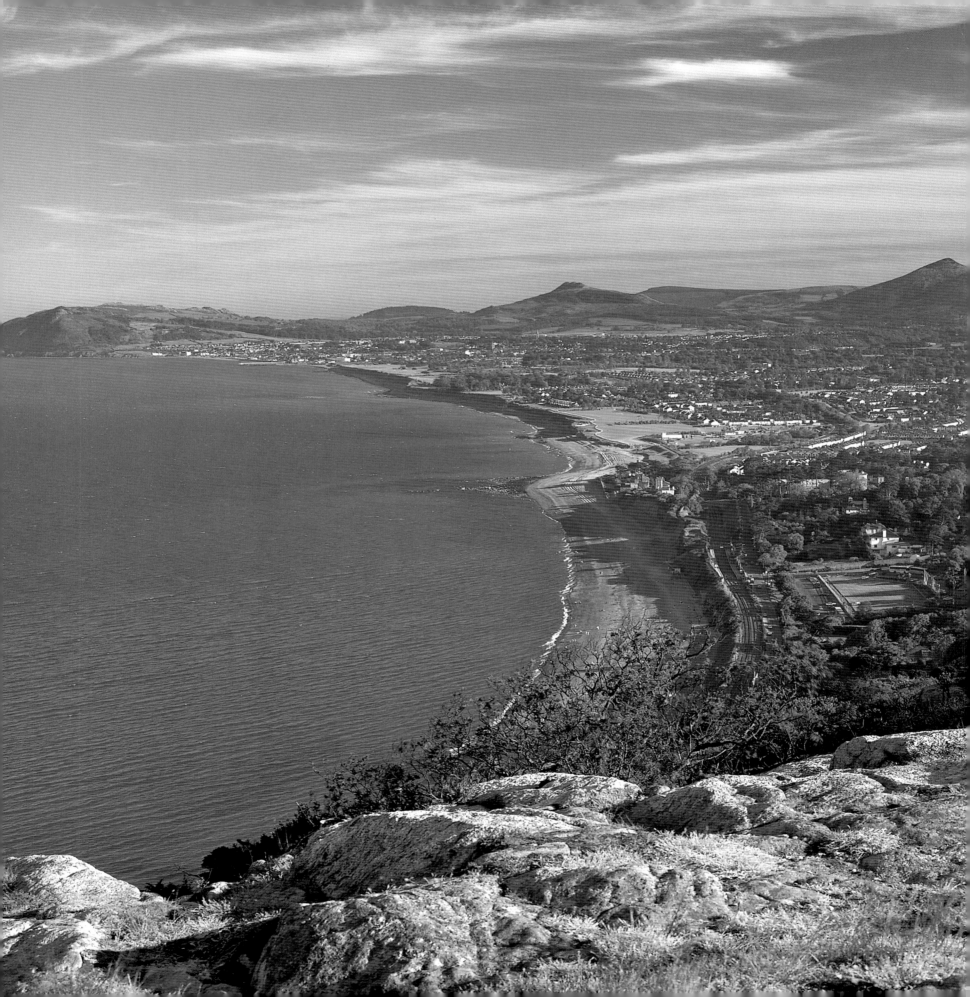

Always remember to forget

The things that made you sad.

But never forget to remember

The things that made you glad.

Always remember to forget

The friends that proved untrue.

But never forget to remember

Those that have stuck by you.

Always remember to forget

The troubles that passed away.

But never forget to remember

The blessings that come each day.

Photography
Credits